God's Favourite Number

AF374547

While every precaution has been taken in the preparation of this book, the publisher assumes no responsibility for errors or omissions, or for damages resulting from the use of the information contained herein.

GOD'S FAVOURITE NUMBER

First edition. July 24, 2024.

Copyright © 2024 Jonathan Blow.

ISBN: 979-8227889294

Written by Jonathan Blow.

<u>Preface</u>

Numbers are an integral part of our lives.
Our age, dates, times all define our lives in everything we do.

The Bible is also dominated by numbers.

Even Satan has a number -
<u>In Revelations 13:18</u> -

"This calls for wisdom. Whoever is.
intelligent can work out the meaning of
the number of the beast, because the
number stands for a man's name. It's
number is 666."

But what is God's favourite number?

The number *forty* appears a few times, for eg -
<u>In Genesis 7:11-12</u> -

When Noah was six hundred years old,
on the <u>seventeen</u> day of the second
month all the outlets of the vast body of
water beneath the earth burst open, all
the floodgates of the sky were opened,
and rain fell on the earth for *forty* days
and nights.

<u>In Matthew 4:1-2</u>

Then the Spirit led Jesus into the desert

1

to be tempted by the Devil. After
spending *forty* days and nights without
food, Jesus was hungry.

The number *twelve* also appears a few times -
<u>In Genesis 49:28</u>

These are the *twelve* tribes of Israel, and
this is what their father said as he spoke
a suitable word of farewell to each son.

<u>In Luke 5:13</u>

When day came, he called his disciples to him and
chose *twelve* of them, whom he named apostles.

The number three also has lots of appearances - <u>In John
14:38</u>

Jesus answered, "Are you really ready to
die for me? I am telling you the truth:
before the cock crows you will say *three*
times that you do not know me.

<u>In Mark 9:30-31</u>

Jesus and his disciples left that place and
went on through Galilee. Jesus did not
want anyone to know where he was,

because he was teaching his disciples:
"The Son of Man will be handed over to
men who kill him. *Three* days later,
however, he will rise to life."
But the number that stands out from all
the rest is the number *__seven__* and *__seven__* is
one more than six, so God is greater and
more powerful than Satan.

In our world there are *__seven__* continents,
__seven__ classical planets, *__seven__* wonders of
the world, seven deadly sins and the list
goes on and on.
There are *__seven__* colors in a rainbow.
Red, orange, yellow, green, blue, indigo and violet.
"As a sign of this everlasting covenant
which I am making with you and with all
my living beings, I am putting my bow in
the clouds."
(Genesis 9:12-13)
David says in Psalms 119:169, "*__Seven__* times each day I thank
you for your righteous judgement"
So this book is all about the number *__seven__*.
How it is used in different stories and contexts and teachings.
My life has been about numbers.
I was an accountant for 30 years, where
numbers are used daily.
Numbers which help to balance and can
be interpreted to tell a story.

The evil part of my life also involved numbers.

I was a gambling addict for a long time.

I got hooked on games particularly roulette which is all about numbers. Numbers which have relationships with

each other.

These relationships drove me crazy trying to find the perfect system. Gambling is also driven by money and

money is all about numbers.

My story is detailed in my book "Default Settings".

In this book I have used the Scripture contained in the Good News Bible —Today's English Version —

British usage edition — First South African Edition, 1977.

Thank you for reading the book.

God Bless You

Jonathan

The Sabbath

This book starts at the beginning. When God created the universe.....

The Lord created light and darkness, the
sky, the earth, sea and plants, the sun,
moon and stars, sea creatures and birds,
animals and human beings, and by the
seventh day God had finished what he had
been doing and stopped working.
He **blessed** the _seventh_ day and set it apart as a **special** day,
because by that day he had completed his creation and
stopped working.
(Genesis 1:3-31; Genesis 2:1-3)
"Observe the Sabbath and keep it **holy**. You have six days in
which you do your work but the _seventh_ day is a day of rest
dedicated to me. On that day nobody is to work - neither
you, nor your children, your slaves, your animals or the
foreigners living in your country. In six days I, the Lord,
made the earth, the sky, the sea, and everything in them but
on the _seventh_ day I rested. That is why, I, the Lord, **blessed**
the Sabbath and made it **holy**."
(Exodus 20: 8-11) (Deuteronomy 5: 12-15)
.The Lord commanded Moses to say to
the people of Israel: "Keep the Sabbath,
_m_y day of rest, because it is a _sign_
between you and me for _all_ time to come,
to show that I, the Lord, have made you

my own people. You must keep the day
of rest, because it is <u>sacred</u>. Whoever
does not keep it and works on that day, is
to be put to death. You have six days in
which to do your work but the *seventh*
day is a <u>solemn</u> day of rest decided by
me."
(Exodus 31: 12-15)

So the Sabbath, the ***seventh*** day of the week, is the Lord's day
of rest. A sign between the Lord and us for all time to come.

It is a holy, sacred and solemn day.

"Do not even light a fire on the Sabbath."
(Exodus 35:3)
While the Israelites were still in the wilderness, a man was
found collecting firewood on the Sabbath. He was taken to
Moses, Aaron and the entire community. He was kept under
guard as it was not certain as to what should be done to
him. But the Lord decided. He said to Moses,
"The man must be put to death. The whole community is to
stone him to death outside the camp. And that's what
happened. The man was stoned to death by the whole
community."
(Numbers 15: 32-36)

And Jesus concluded,
"The Sabbath was made for the good of man; man was not made for the Sabbath. So the Son of Man is Lord even on the Sabbath."
(Mark 2:27)

It is clear that the Lord chose his day of rest, His holy day, His sacred day, His solemn day, as the _seventh_ day of the week.

It was made for the good of man.

Of all the days, the Lord chose the _seventh_ - God's favourite number!

Cain [1]

After Adam and Eve were sent out of the
    Garden of Eden they were made to
    cultivate the soil from which they had
    been formed.

Then Adam had intercourse with his wife and she became
pregnant....

Adam and Eve had two children.

Cain (meaning acquired) and Abel (meaning breath). Cain
became a farmer and Abel a shepherd.

After some time Cain brought some of his harvest and gave
it as an offering to the Lord.

Abel, however, brought the first born
lamb of one of his sheep, killed it and
gave the best parts of it as an offering.
It was Faith that made Abel offer to God a better sacrifice
than Cain's. Through his faith he won God's approval as a
righteous man, because God himself approved of his gifts.
By means of his faith Abel still speaks, even though he is
dead.
(Hebrews 11:4)

The Lord was pleased with Abel and his offering, but he
rejected Cain's offering. Cain became furious and scowled in
anger.

The Lord said to Cain,

"Why are you angry? What is with the
scowl on your face? If you had done the
right thing you would be smiling and I
would have accepted your offering. But
because you have done evil, sin is
crouching at your door. It wants to rule
you but you must overcome it."

Then Cain said to his brother Abel, "Let us go out into the
fields".
When they were out in the fields Cain
turned on his brother and killed him.

As a result, the punishment for the
murder of all innocent men will fall on
you, from the murder of innocent Abel to
the murder of Zachariah son of
Berachiah, whom you murdered between
the Temple and the altar.
(Matthew 23:35)
We must not be like Cain: He belonged to the Evil One and
murdered his own brother Abel. Why did Cain murder
him?
Because the things he himself did were wrong, but the
things his brother did were right. (1 John 3:12)

The Lord asked him,
"Where is your brother Abel?

Cain replied,

"I don't know. Am I supposed to take care of my brother?"
Then the Lord said,

"Why have you done this terrible thing?
Your brother's blood is crying out to me
from the ground, like a voice calling for
revenge. You, Cain, are placed under a
curse and can no longer farm the soil. It
has soaked up your brother's blood as if
it had opened its mouth to receive it
when you killed him.
You have come to Jesus, who arranged the new covenant,
and to the sprinkled blood that promises much better things
than does the blood of Abel.
(Hebrews 12:24)

If you try to grow crops, the soil will not produce anything;
you will be a homeless wanderer on earth." Cain replied,

" The punishment is too hard for me to
bear. You are driving me off the land and
away from your presence. I will be a
homeless wanderer on earth, and anyone
whoever finds me will kill me."

But the Lord answered,
"NO. If anyone kills you, **_seven_** lives will be taken in
revenge."
So the Lord put a mark on Cain to warn anyone who met
him not to kill him.

Cain and his wife had another son and named him Enoch. Enoch's great great grandfather was Lamech.

Lamech said to his wives,

"Adah and Zillah, listen to me: I have killed a young man because he struck me.

.If _seven_ lives are taken to pay for killing Cain, **_Seventy-seven_** will be taken if anyone kills me."

Then Peter came to Jesus and asked,
."Lord, if my brother keeps on sinning against me, how many times do I have to forgive him? _Seven times_?" "No, not _seven_ times," answered Jesus, "but _seventy_ times _seven_ because the Kingdom of heaven is like this.
Once there was a king who decided to check on his servants' accounts. He had just begun to do so when one of them was brought in who owed him millions of pounds.
The servant did not have enough to pay his debt, so the king ordered him to be sold as a slave, with his wife and his children and all that he had, in order to pay the debt. The servant fell on his knees before the king. 'Be patient with me,' he begged, ' and I will pay you everything!'
The king felt sorry for him, so he forgave him his debt and he let him go. Then the man went out and met one of his fellow-servants who owed him a few pounds. He grabbed him and started choking him.
'Pay back what you owe me!' He said.
His fellow-servant fell down and begged him,

'Be patient with me, and I will pay you back!'
But he refused; instead he had him thrown into jail until he could pay the debt. When the other servants saw what had happened, they were very upset and went to the king and told him everything. So he called the servant in.
'You worthless slave!' He said. 'I forgave you the whole amount you owed me, just because you asked me to. You should have had mercy on your fellow-servant just as I had mercy on you.' The king was very angry, and he sent the servant to jail to be punished until he should pay back the whole amount."
And Jesus concluded,

"That is how my Father in heaven will treat every one of you unless you forgive your brother from your heart."
(Matthew 18: 21-35)

So the Lord used the number as a warning to the people and so did Cain's descendant Lamech. The number **_seven_** - God's favourite number!

[1] This story is taken from Genesis Chapter 4

Noah [1]

Noah (meaning relief) was the son of Lamech.
When Noah was alive, everyone on earth was wicked. The
Lord said,

"I will wipe out these people I have
created, and also the animals and the
birds, because I am sorry that I made any
of them."

But the Lord was pleased with Noah...

Noah had no faults and was the only
good man of his time. He lived in
fellowship with God, but everyone else
was evil in God's sight and violence had
spread everywhere.

The people were all living evil lives. God said to Noah,

"I have decided to put an end to all
mankind. I will destroy them completely
because the world is full of their violent
deeds. Build a boat for yourself out of
good timber. I am going to send a flood
on the earth to destroy every living
being. Everything on earth will die, but I
will make a covenant with you. Go into
the boat with your wife, your sons and
their wives (Noah had three sons. So it
was Noah plus _**seven**_ people)

God did not spare the ancient world, but brought the flood on the world of godless people; the only ones he saved were Noah, who preached righteousness, and _seven_ other people.
(2 Peter 2:5)

Take into the boat with you a male and
female of each kind of animal and every
kind of bird, in order to keep them alive.
Take along all kinds of food for you and
them."

Noah did everything that the Lord commanded.

The Lord continued, "Take with you
seven pairs of each kind of ritually clean
animal, but only one pair of each kind of
unclean animal. Take with also _seven_
pairs of each kind of bird. _Seven_ days
from now I am going to send rain that
will fall for forty days and nights, in
order to destroy all living beings I have
made,"
All the outlets of the vast body of water
between the earth began to open and all
the floodgates of the sky were opened
and rain fell for forty days and nights.

And it was also by water, the water of the flood, that the old world was destroyed.
(2 Peter 3:6)

The water became deeper and the boat
drifted on the surface. It became so deep
that it covered the highest mountains. It
went on rising until it was _seven_ meters

above the tops of the mountains. Every
living being on the earth died - every
bird, every animal and every person.
The only ones left were Noah and those who were living with him
on the boat.

Jesus said,
"The coming of the Son of Man will be like what happened
in the time of Noah. In the days before the flood the people
ate and drank, men and women married, up to the very day
Noah went into the boat; yet they did not realize what was
happening until the flood came and swept them all away.
That is how it will be when the Son of Man comes."
(Matthew 24:37-39)
The rain stopped and the water gradually went down for
150 days. On the seventeenth day of the seventh
month the boat came to rest on a
mountain in the Ararat range.
After forty days Noah opened a window
and sent out a raven. It did not come
back, but kept flying around until the
water was completely gone. Meanwhile
Noah sent out a dove to see if the water
was going down, but since the water still
covered the land the dove did not find
anywhere to alight. It flew back to the
boat. Noah waited another **_seven_** days and
sent the dove out again. It returned to
him in the evening with a fresh olive leaf

in its beak. So Noah knew that the water
had gone down. Then he waited another
**seven** days and sent out the dove once
again; this time it did not come back.

By the twenty _**seventh**_ day of the 2nd month the earth
was completely dry. The Lord said to
himself,

"Never again will I put the earth under a
curse because of what man does; I know
that from the time he is young his
thoughts are evil. Never again will I
destroy all living beings as I have done
this time. As long as the world exists,
there will be a time for planting and a
time for harvest. There will always be
cold and heat, summer and winter, day
and night!"

Noah and the _**seven**_ other people were saved.

God decided to save them and _**seven**_ pairs of ritually
clean animals. God decided on the number
- God's favourite number.

[1]This story comes from Genesis Chapters 6 - 9.

Jacob and Rachel [1]

Isaac was the son of Abraham.

Isaac had two sons, Jacob (meaning heel) and Esau (meaning hairy) Esau hated Jacob, because his father had given Jacob his blessing.

Rebecca, their mother, was worried that Esau would kill Jacob, so she devised a plan to send him away.....

Rebecca (Isaac's wife) said to Isaac one day,

"I am sick and tired of Esau's foreign
wives. If Jacob also marries one of these
Hittite girls, I might as well die."

Isaac then called Jacob and said to him,

"Don't marry a Canaanite girl. Go instead
to Mesopotamia to the home of your
grandfather Bethuel and marry one of
the girls there, one of your uncle Laban's
daughters."

Laban was the son of Bethuel the Aramean and the brother of Rebecca. So Jacob did as Isaac said.

Jacob came upon a well out in the fields with three flocks of sheep lying around.

The shepherds spoke to Jacob who were
from Hanan. They pointed out Rachel
who was on her way to the well with her

dad's flock of sheep.
When Jacob saw Rachel with his uncle
Laban's flock he went to the well, rolled
the stone back in front of the well and
watered the sheep. Then he kissed her
and began to cry with joy.

He said to her,

"I am your fathers relative, the son of
Rebecca." Rebecca ran to tell her father
who went to meet Jacob, hugged him and
kissed him and brought him into his
house. Jacob told Laban everything that
happened and Laban replied,

"Yes indeed you are my own flesh and blood."

Jacob stayed for a whole month. Laban said to Jacob,

"You shouldn't work for me for nothing just because you are
my relative. How much pay do you want?"

Now Laban had two daughters, the elder
one was Leah. Leah had lovely eyes but
Rachel was shapely and beautiful.

Jacob was in love with Rachel, so he said,

"I will work **_seven_** years for you, if you let me marry Rachel."
Laban agreed and said,

"I would rather give her to you then anyone else, stay here
with me."

Jacob worked for **_seven_** years so he could
have Rachel and the time seemed like a
few days to him, because he loved her.

The time passed and Jacob said to Laban,

"The time is up, let me marry your daughter."

So Laban gave a wedding-feast and
invited everyone. But that night instead
of Rachel, he took Leah to Jacob and
Jacob had intercourse with her. The next
morning Jacob discovered it was Leah
and not Rachel. He went to Laban and
asked him why he had tricked him.

Laban answered,

"It is not the custom here to give your
younger daughter in marriage before the
elder. Wait until this week's marriage
celebrations are over, and I will give you
Rachel, if you will work for me for
another **_seven_** years."
Jacob agreed and once the marriage
celebrations were over, Laban gave
Rachel to him as his wife. Jacob had
intercourse with Rachel also, and he
loved her more than Leah.

Then he worked for Laban for another **_seven_** years.

Jacob and Leah had children:

Reuben - meaning the Lord has seen my troubles and now
my husband will love me;

Simeon - meaning the Lord heard I was not loved;

Levi - meaning now my husband will be bound more tightly
to me;

Judah - meaning praise the Lord.

Rachel became jealous of her sister as
she couldn't have children. So she gave
Jacob her slave girl Bilhah to sleep with,
so she could become a mother through
her.
Bilhah had two sons and Rachel named
the first one Dan - meaning God has
judged in my favor and the second one
Naphtali - meaning I have fought a hard
fight with my sister and I have won.
Leah realized she had stopped having
children so she gave her slave girl Zilpah
as his wife and she bore him a son, who
Leah named Gad - meaning lucky - and
another son named Asher - meaning
happy.
Leah gave Rachel mandrakes which her
son had brought for her and Rachel
allowed her to sleep with Jacob again. She
bore him another son called Issachar -
meaning reward - and then another son
named Zebulun - meaning fine gift.

Later on she had a daughter named Dinah - meaning God
will judge. So Leah had ___seven___ kids - 6 sons and 1 daughter.

God remembered Rachel and he
answered her prayer, so she became

pregnant and gave birth to Joseph -
meaning God has taken away my
disgrace, and Benjamin - meaning son
who will be fortunate.

After Benjamin was born Rachel died.

The meanings of the names of the sons and daughter of
Jacob can be used as a prayer to the Lord, as follows:

> ***God has seen my troubles,***
> ***God has heard me,***
> ***He has bound us more tightly,***
> ***Praise the Lord,***

> ***He judges in our favour,***

> ***He fought a hard fight and won,***
> ***I am lucky,***
> ***I am happy,***
> ***As God has rewarded me,***
> ***And has given me a fine gift,***
> ***God will judge,***
> ***And take away my disgrace,***
> ***I will be forever fortunate.***
> ***Amen***

Jacob asked Laban if he could go back home after Joseph was
born.

Jacob has become very wealthy, he had many flocks, slaves,
camels and donkeys.

Laban and his sons were no longer friendly with Jacob as they accused him of taking all their wealth. The Lord said to Jacob,

"Go back to the land of your father and relatives and I will be with you." Rachel and Leah agreed and said,

"Our father has nothing left for us to inherit and he treats us like foreigners. All the wealth that God has taken from our father belongs to us and our children.

Do whatever God has told you!"

Jacob put his children and wives on the camels and drove his flocks back to Canaan. Jacob did not let Laban know he was going.

Three days later after Jacob had.
left, Laban was told that they had
fled. Laban took his men and
pursued after Jacob for

seven days until he caught up with him in Gilead.

Laban and Jacob made an agreement. Laban said,

"May the Lord keep an eye on us while we are separated from each other. If you ill-treat my daughters or if you marry

other women, remember that God is watching even though I don't know about it!"

So Jacob worked for years to get his wife, the love of his life. The number of years he worked for was God's favourite number!

[1] This story is taken from Genesis Chapters 28-31

—————————Joseph and king of Egypt [1]

Joseph's brothers were jealous of him and they plotted against him and decided to kill him.

But Reuben, the oldest brother,
persuaded them not to kill Joseph, but
rather to throw him in a well. They
changed their minds and rather sold him
for twenty pieces of silver to the
Ishmaelites, who took him to Egypt.

Joseph ended up in prison and in prison he interpreted the
prisoner's dreams.

The king of Egypt found out about this and sent for Joseph
to interpret his dreams....

The King of Egypt one night dreamt he
was standing by the river Nile, when
seven fat and sleek cows came out of the
river and began to feed on the grass.
Then _seven_ other cows, thin and bony,
came and stood with the other cows on
the river bank. The thin cows ate up the
fat cows. The King woke up. He fell
asleep again and had another dream.
Seven ears of corn, full and ripe, were
growing on one stalk. Then _seven_ other

ears of corn sprouted thin and scorched
by the desert wind and the thin ears of
corn swallowed up the full ones. The
King woke up and realized he had been
dreaming.

In the morning he was worried about the dream and sent for
all the wise men and magicians of Egypt.

"So the King sent for his fortune-tellers,
magicians, sorcerers and wizards to
come and explain the dream to him."
(Daniel 2:2)

But not one of them could explain the
dreams to him. A wine steward told the
King about a young Hebrew who had
interpreted his dream for him. Things
had turned out just as he said. The King
sent for Joseph and said to him,

"I have had a dream and nobody can explain it and I have
been told that you can interpret dreams." The King told the
dream to Joseph.

Joseph explained,

"The two dreams mean the same thing,
God has told you what he is going to do.
The _**seven**_ fat cows and the _**seven**_ full ears
of corn are _**seven**_ years of feast - they
have the same meaning. The _**seven**_ thin
cows and _**seven**_ thin ears are _**seven**_ years
of famine. God has shown you what he is

going to do. There will be **_seven_** years of great plenty in Egypt. After **_seven_** years of plenty, there will be **_seven_** years of famine and all the good years will be forgotten, because the famine will ruin the country. The repetition of your dreams means that the matter is fixed by God and that he will make it happen in the future.

Now you will need to choose some <u>man</u> with wisdom and insight and put him in charge of the country. You must also appoint other officials and take a fifth of the crops during the **_seven_** years of plenty. Order them to collect all the food during the good years that are coming and give the authority to store up corn in the cities and guard it. The food will be a reserve supply for the country during the **_seven_** years of famine which are going to come to Egypt. By doing this the children will not starve.

The King said to Joseph,

"God has shown you all this so it is obvious that you have greater wisdom and insight than anyone else. I will put you in charge of my country and all my people will obey your orders. Your authority will be only second

only to mine. I will now appoint you Governor over all Egypt."
"Immediately Belshazzar ordered his servants to dress
Daniel in a robe of royal purple and hang a gold chain of
honor around his neck. And he made him the third in
power in his kingdom."
(Daniel 5:29)
"When Joseph appeared before the King of Egypt, God gave
him a pleasing manner and wisdom, and the king made
Joseph governor over the country and the royal household. "
(Acts 7:10)

Joseph was given the name Zaphenath Paneah, and gave him
a wife, a daughter of a priest, Asenath.

During the **_seven_** years of plenty the land
produced abundant crops and Joseph
collected the crops and stored them in
the cities.

There was so much corn, like the sand of the sea.

Joseph had two sons during the **_seven_** years of plenty.

Manasseh (meaning God has made me forget all my
sufferings) and Ephraim (meaning God has given me
children in the land of my trouble)

When the **_seven_** years of plenty ended, the **_seven_** years of
famine began.

"Then there was a famine all over Egypt and Canaan, which
caused much suffering. Our ancestors could not find any
food."
(Acts 7:11)

There was no food in any country except
Egypt. Joseph opened all the storehouses
and sold corn to all the Egyptians.

People came to Egypt from all over the world to buy corn
from Joseph. Joseph, through God, saved the people of
Egypt from starvation!

[1] This story is taken from Genesis Chapter 41

The death of Jacob [1]

Jacob lived in Egypt for **_seventeen_** years, until he was a hundred and forty _seven_ years old. But the time had come for him to die.....

Jacob said to Joseph,

"As you see, I am about to die, but God
    will be with you and will take you back to
    the land of your ancestors. It is you and
    not your brothers that I am giving
    Shechem, the fertile region which I took
    from the Ammonites with my sword and
    my bow."

Then Jacob called his sons and said,

"Gather round and I will tell you what you what will happen
to you in the future:-

• <u>Rueben</u> : You are my first born, you
are my strength. You are like.
a raging flood, but you will
not be the most important;

• <u>Simeon & Levi</u> : You will be scattered

throughout the land of
Israel;

• <u>Judah</u> : You are like a lion. Your descendants will always
rule;

"The nation is like a mighty lion.; When it is sleeping, no
one dares wake it; Whoever blesses Israel will be blessed;
And whoever curses Israel will be cursed."
(Numbers 24:9)
"Then one of the elders said to me,
'Don't cry. Look! The Lion from Judah's tribe, the great
descendant of David, has won the victory, and he can break
the _seven_ seals and open the scroll."
(Revelations 5:5)

- Zebulam : You will live besides the sea;
- Issachar : You will be forced to work

like a slave;

- Dan : You will be a ruler for the people;
- Gad : You will be attacked by a band of

robbers;

- Asher : Your land will produce rich

food;

- Naphtali : You are a deer that runs free;
- Joseph : The Almighty God will bless

you and set you apart from
your brothers;

- Benjamin : You are like a vicious wolf,

killing and devouring.

Jacob commanded his sons to bury him
in the same place as Abraham and Sarah,
Isaac and Rebecca and his wife Leah.

Jacob died once he had finished giving instructions.

Joseph, all the King's officials, the senior
men of his court and all the leading men
of Egypt went to bury his father. Along
with Joseph's family, his brothers and
the rest of Jacob's family.
When they arrived at the threshing place they mourned loudly for
a long time and Joseph performed mourning
ceremonies for **_seven_** days.
The citizens of Canaan saw the people mourning and said,
"What a solemn ceremony of mourning the Egyptians are holding."
That is why the place was known as Abel Mizraim meaning
mourning of the Egyptians. Joseph and his brothers
buried their father in the cave at Machpelah.

"Then Jacob went to Egypt, where he and
his sons died. Their bodies were taken to
Shechem, where they were buried in the
grave which Abraham had bought from
the clan of Hamor for a sum of money."
(Acts 7: 15-16)

Joseph and all the people mourned for
seven days to say goodbye to the great
man Jacob - they decided to use God's
Favourite number.

[1] This story is taken from Genesis Chapters 49-50

_Moses' escape [1]

Moses was hidden in a basket in the tall
grass at the edge of the river. This was to
keep him from being killed, as the king of
Egypt had issued a command that every
new-born Hebrew boy was to be thrown
in the Nile.

Moses was saved by the King's daughter and was adopted as
her own son....

When Moses had grown up, he went out
to visit his people, the Hebrews, and he
saw how they were forced to do hard
labour.

He even saw an Egyptian kill an Hebrew.

Moses looked all around and when he
saw nobody was watching, he killed the
Egyptian and buried his body in the sand.

The next day he went back and saw two Hebrew men
fighting. He said to the one in the wrong,

"Why are you beating up a fellow-Hebrew?" The man
answered,

"Who made you our ruler and judge?

Are you going to kill me just like you killed the Egyptian
yesterday?"

Then Moses was afraid as he knew the people had found out what he had done.

> "When Moses was 40 years old, he decided to find out how his fellow-Israelites were being treated. He saw one of them being ill-treated by an Egyptian, so he went to his help and took revenge on the Egyptian by killing him (He thought his own people would understand that God was going to use him to set them free, but they did not understand). The next day he saw two Israelites fighting, and he tried to make peace between them. 'Listen men', he said, 'You are fellow-Israelites; why are you fighting like this? But the one who was ill-treating the other pushed Moses aside. 'Who made you ruler and judge over us?' He asked. 'Do you want to kill me, just as you killed that Egyptian yesterday? When Moses heard this, he fled from Egypt and went to live in the land of Midian. There he had two sons."
> (Acts 7: 23-29)

The King did find out and tried to have Moses killed. But Moses fled and went to live in the land of Midian.

"It was Faith that made Moses, when he had grown up,
refuse to be called the son of the King's daughter. He
preferred to suffer with God's people rather than to enjoy
sin for a little while. He reckoned that to suffer scorn for the
Messiah was worth far more than all the treasures of Egypt,
for he kept his eyes on the future reward."
(Hebrews 11:24-25)

One day Moses was sitting by a well.

The **_Seven_** daughters of the priest of
Midian, Jethro, came to the well to draw
water and fill their troughs for their
father's sheep and goats.
Shepherds drove Jethro's daughters away but Moses rescued them
and watered their animals for them. The
daughters told Jethro about what Moses had done and Jethro
invited Moses to live with them.
Jethro gave Moses one of his **_seven_** daughters to marry.
Her name was Zipporah, she bore Moses a son named Gersham,
meaning I am a foreigner in this land.
So Moses met his wife and married her, one of **_seven_** daughters!
God's favourite number influenced Moses, a prophet second to
none in Israel!
[1] This story is taken from Exodus Chapter 2

Festivals [1]

The Lord gave Moses the following
regulations for the religious festivals,
when the people of Israel are to gather
for worship....

**The festival of unleavened
bread(Passover) (Food offering)**
The Lord said,

"For *seven* days you must eat only
unleavened bread, that is bread not made
with yeast. On the first day you are to get
rid of all the yeast in your houses, for if
anyone during those *seven* days eats
bread made with yeast, he shall no longer
be considered one of my people.
On the first day and again on the *seventh*
day you are to meet for worship. No work
is to be done on these days but you may
prepare food. Keep this festival, because
it is on this day that I brought your tribes
out of Egypt. For all time to come you
must celebrate this day as a festival. For
seven days no yeast must be found in
your house, for if anyone, native-born or
foreign eats bread made with yeast, he
shall no longer be considered one of my
people."
Offer your food offerings to the Lord for
seven days, but on the *seventh* day you

shall again gather for worship, but you shall do none of your daily work.

The Harvest festival (Pentecost)

Count **_seven_** full weeks from the day after the Sabbath day on which you bring your sheaf of corn to present to the Lord. On the fifteenth day present to the Lord another new offering of corn. Each family is to bring two loaves of bread and present them to the Lord as a special gift. And with the bread the community is to present **_seven_** one-year old lambs, one bull, and two goats none of which may have any defects. They shall be offered as a burnt offering to the Lord, together with the grain offering and a wine offering. Also offer one male goat as a sin offering and two one-year old male lambs as a fellowship offering. These offerings are holy. On that day do none of your daily work, but gather for worship. Your descendants are to observe this regulation for all time to come. No matter where they live.

When you harvest your fields do not cut the corn at the edges of the fields, and do not go back to cut the ears of the corn at the edges of the fields, and do not go back to cut the ears of the corn that were left, leave them for the poor people and foreigners. The Lord is your God.

New years festival

On the first day of the **_seventh_** month observe a special day of rest, and come together for worship, when the trumpet sounds. Present a food-offering to the Lord and do none of your daily work.

<u>Day of Atonement</u>

The tenth day of the **<u>seventh</u>** month is the day when the annual ritual is to be performed to take away the sins of the people. On that day do not eat anything at all, come together for worship and present a food offering to the Lord. Do not work on that day, because it is the day for performing the ritual to take away sins. This regulation applies to your descendants no matter where they live.

<u>The festival of shelters</u>

The festival of shelters begins on the fifteenth day of the **<u>seventh</u>** month, and continues for **<u>seven</u>** days. Each day for **<u>seven</u>** days you shall present a food-offering.

These festivals are in addition to the regular Sabbath.

When you have harvested your fields, celebrate this festival for **<u>seven</u>** days. The first day shall be a special day of rest.

On that day take some of the best fruit from your trees, the palm branches and the branches of leafy trees and begin a religious festival to honor the Lord your God. Celebrate it for several days. All the people of Israel shall live in shelters for **<u>seven</u>** *days*.

<u>Offerings for unintentional sins</u>

If it is the whole community of Israel
that sins and becomes guilty of breaking
one of the Lord's commands without
intending to, then as soon as the sin
becomes known, the community shall
bring a young bull as a sin offering. They
shall bring it to the Tent of the Lord's
Presence. The leaders of the community
shall put their hands on its head and it
shall be killed there. The High Priest
shall take some of the bull's blood into
the Tent, dip his finger in it and sprinkle
it in front of the curtain **_seven_** times.

In this way he shall make the sacrifice for the people's sins and they will be FORGIVEN. So all the Lord's festivals included his number - God's number!

[1] This story is taken from Leviticus Chapter 2

Moses on Mount Sinai [1]

The people of Israel left Rephidim, and
on the first day of the third month after
they had left Egypt they came to the
desert of Sinai.

There they set up camp at the foot of Mount Sinai and
Moses went up the mountain to meet with God.....

The Lord said to Moses,

"Come up the mountain to me and while
you are here I will give you the two stone
tablets which control all the laws that I
have written for the instructions of the
people."

Moses and his helper Joshua got ready and they began to go
up the mountain. Before he left, Moses said to the leaders,

"Wait here in the camp for us until we
come back. Aaron and Hur are here with
you and so whoever has a dispute to
settle can go with them."

They went up Mount Sinai and a cloud covered it.

The dazzling light of the Lord's presence came down onto
the mountain. To the Isrealites the light looked like a fire
burning on top of the mountain.

The cloud covered the mountain for six days and on the **_seventh_** day the Lord called Moses from the cloud. Moses went up on the mountain into the cloud.

There he stayed for 40 days and nights.

The Lord called Moses on his day, God's favourite number!
[1] This story comes from Exodus Chapter 24

——The lamp-stand [1]

The Lord said to Moses,

"The people must make a Sacred Tent for me, so that I may live among them. Make it and all the furnishings

according to the plans I will show you. Make a lamp-stand of pure gold. Make its base and its shaft out of

hammered gold; its decorative flowers, including buds and petals, are to form one piece with it. Six branches

shall extend from its sides, three from each side. Each of the six branches is to have three decorative flowers

shaped like almond blossoms with buds and petals. The shaft of the lamp-stand is to have four decorative

shapes like almond blossoms with buds and petals. There is to be one bud below each of the three pairs of

branches.

The buds, the branches and the lamp-stand are to be a single piece of pure hammered gold. Make _seven_ lamps

for the lamp-stand and set them up so that they shine towards the front. Make its tongs and tray of pure gold.

Use 35 kgs of pure gold to make the lamp-stand and all its equipment. Take care to make them according to the

plan that I showed you on the mountain.

The angel who had been speaking to me came again and roused me as if I had been sleeping. "What do you see?" He asked.

"A lamp-stand made of gold," I answered. "At the top is a bowl for the oil. On the lamp-stand are _seven_ lamps, each one with places for _seven_ wicks."

The angel said to me,

"The _seven_ lamps are the _seven_ eyes of the Lord, which see all over the earth."
(Zechariah 4:1-10b)
The instructions for the making of the lamp-stand included God's favourite number and that number is also the number of eyes of the Lord.

[1] This story comes from Exodus Chapter 25

Ordaining of Priests [1]

"Bring Aaron and his sons to the front of the Tent of my Presence and tell them to take a ritual bath. Dress

Aaron in his priestly garments. Put the turban on him and tie on it the sacred sign of dedication,engraved,

'dedicated to the Lord.'

Then take the anointing oil, pour it on his head and anoint him. Bring his sons and put shirts on them, put

sashes around their waists and tie caps on their heads. Them and their descendants are to serve me as

priests forever. Sacrifice the bull and the rams and sacrifice as burnt offerings to me.

"Your life must be controlled by love, just as Christ loved us
and gave his life for us as a sweet-smelling offering and
sacrifice that pleases God."
(Ephesians 5:2)

"Here, then, is my receipt for everything you have given me -
and it has been more than enough! I have all I need now
that Epaphroditus has brought me all your gifts. They are
like a sweet-smelling offering to God, a sacrifice which is
acceptable and pleasing to him."
(Phillipians 4:18)

When a priest is ordained, the breast and the thigh of the ram being used for the ordination are to be dedicated

to me as a special gift and set aside for the priests. It is my unchanging decision that when my people make their fellowship offerings, the breast and the thigh of the animal belong to the priests. This is the people's gift

to me, the Lord.

Aaron's priestly garments are to be handed onto his sons after his death for them to wear when they are

ordained. The son of Aaron who succeeds him as priest and who goes into the Tent of my Presence to serve in

the Holy Place is to wear these garments for _**seven**_ days.

Perform the rites of ordination for Aaron and his sons for _**seven**_ days exactly as I have commanded you. Each day you must offer a bull as a sacrifice, so that sin may be forgiven.

This will purify the altar.

Then anoint it with olive oil to make it holy. Do this every day for _**seven**_ days.

Then the altar will be completely holy and anyone or anything that touches it will be harmed by the power of its

holiness!!!

God's commands were clear about the ordaining of his sacred Priests - the rites must be performed for _**seven**_

days and the altar must be purified for _**seven**_ days.

God's favourite number.

[1] This story is taken from Exodus Chapter 29

Rules and Regulations [1]

Moses wrote down God's Law and gave it to the Levitical priests who were in charge of the Lord's Covenant Box,
   and to the leaders of Israel.

   He commanded them,

"At the end of every _seven_ years, when the year that debts are canceled comes around, read this aloud at the
   Festival of Shelters.

   Read it to the people of Israel when they come to worship
   the Lord your God at the one place of worship.

   Call together all the men, women and children, and the foreigners who live in your towns, so that everyone
   may hear it and learn to honor the Lord your God and to obey his teachings faithfully.

   In this way your descendants who have never heard the Law
   of the Lord your God, will hear it.

   And so they will learn to obey him as long as they live in the
   land you are about to occupy across the Jordan. The Law was
   read every _seven_ years - according to God's command.

The treatment and release of slaves [2]

   If you buy a Hebrew slave, he shall serve you for six years. In the _seventh_ year he is to be set free without having
   to pay anything. If he was unmarried when he became your slave, he is not to take a wife with him when he

leaves, but if he was married when he became your slave, he may take his wife with him. If his master gave him

a wife and she bore him children, the woman and children belong to the master and the man may leave by

himself, but if the slave declares that he loves his master, his wife and his children and he does not want to be

set free, then his master shall take him to the place of worship.

There he is to make him stand against the door/door-post and pierce his ear. Then he will be his slave for life.

So the Lord commanded slaves to be released in **_seven_** years.

If a fellow-Israelite living near you becomes so poor that he sells himself to you as a slave, you shall not make

him do the work of a slave. He shall stay with you as a hired man and serve you for **_seven_** years. At that time he

and his children shall leave you and return to his family and to the property of his ancestors. The people of

Israel are the Lord's slaves. Do not treat them harshly, but fear your God!

Purification of women [3]

For **_seven_** days after a woman gives birth to a son, she is ritually unclean as she is during her monthly period.

On the eighth day the child shall be circumcised.
"Jesus is named. A week later, when the time came for the baby to be circumcised, he was named Jesus, the name which the angel had given him before he had been conceived."
(Luke 2:21)

For fourteen days after she gives birth to a daughter she is ritually unclean. When the time for her purification is
complete she shall bring to the priest at the entrance of the Tent of the Lord's Presence, a one year old lamb as
a burnt offering and a pigeon or a dove for a sin offering.

"They also went to offer a sacrifice of a pair of doves or two
young pigeons, as required by the Law of the Lord."
(Luke 2:24)

The priest shall present her offering to the Lord and perform the ritual to take away her impurity. When a
woman has her monthly period, she remains unclean for seven days. Anything on where she sits or lies during
her monthly period is unclean.

<u>Skin diseases</u> [4]

If anyone has a sore on his skin or a boil or an inflammation which could develop into a skin-disease, he shall be
brought to the Aaronite Priest. The priest shall examine the sore and if it is a dreaded skin disease, the priest
shall pronounce the person unclean.

If the sore is white and does not appear to be deeper than the skin round it and the hairs have not turned white,
the priest shall isolate the person for **_seven_** days.

The priest shall examine him again on the **_seventh_** day, and if in his opinion the sore looks the same and has not
spread, he shall isolate him for another seven days. The priest shall examine him again on the seventh day and
if the sore has faded and has not spread, he shall pronounce him ritually clean - it is only a sore.

But if the sore spreads after the priest examines him, he must appear before the priest again, and he shall
pronounce him unclean - it is a dreaded skin-disease.

An open sore means a dreaded skin-disease and the person is unclean.

<u>Rules for the Nazarites</u> [5]

The Lord commanded Moses to give the following instructions to the people of Israel. Any man or woman who

makes a special vow to become a Nazirite and dedicates himself to the Lord:

Shall abstain from wine and beer;

He shall not drink any drink from grapes;

He shall not eat anything that comes from a grapevine;

He must not cut his hair or shave his beard for the full time he is dedicated to the Lord;

He must not defile himself by going near a corpse;

He is consecrated to the Lord;

If the hair of a Nazirite is defiled because he is right besides someone who dies, he must wait <u>*seven*</u> days and

then shave off his hair and beard, and so he becomes ritually clean.

The priest shall perform the ritual of purification for him. On the same day the man shall reconsecrate his hair

and rededicate it to the Lord.

The previous period of time does not count because his consecrated hair was defiled.

[1] This story comes from Deuteronomy Chapter 31

[2] These stories come from Exodus Chapter 21 and Leviticus Chapter 25

[3] This story comes from Leviticus Chapter 12

[4] This story comes from Leviticus Chapter 13

[5] This story comes from Numbers Chapter 6

Obedience and Disobedience [1]

The Lord said there are blessings for Obedience and punishment for Disobedience....

<u>Obedience</u>
The Lord said,

"If you live according to my Laws and obey my commands, I will send you rain at the right time, so that the

land will produce crops and the trees will bear fruit. Your crops will be plentiful so you will still be harvesting

corn when it is time to pick grapes, and you will still be picking grapes when it is time to sow corn. You will

have all that you want to eat, and you will live in safety in your land.

1. I will give you peace in your land and you will sleep without being afraid;
2. I will get rid of the dangerous animals in the land and there will be no more war time;
3. You will be victorious over your enemies;
4. I will bless you and give you many children;
5. I will live among you in my Sacred Tent and I will never turn away from you;
6. I will be with you; I will be your God and you will be my people.

As God himself has said,
"I will make my home with my people and live among them;
I will be their God and they shall be my people."
(2 Corinthians 6:16)

I BROKE THE POWER THAT HELD YOU DOWN AND LET YOU WALK WITH YOUR HEAD HELD HIGH.

<u>Disobedience</u>

If you do not obey my commands you will be punished. If you refuse to obey my laws and commands and break

the covenant I have made with you, I will punish you, I will bring disaster on you.

1. Incurable diseases and fevers that will make you blind and cause your life to waste away;

2. You will sow your seed but it will do no good;

3. Your enemies will conquer you and eat what you have grown;

4. Those who hate you will rule over you; you will be so terrified that you will run when no one is chasing

you.

If after all of this you still do not obey me, I will increase your punishment **_seven_** times.

• There will be no rain

If you still continue to resist me, I will again increase your punishment **_seven_** times.

• I will send dangerous animals amongst you - they will kill your children, cattle and leave so few of you that

your roads will be deserted.

If after all of this you still defy me, I will punish you **_seven_** times harder than before:

- war
- diseases
- no food

If after all of this you still defy me, I will punish you a further **_seven_** times harder:

- you will be so hungry you will eat your own children;
- I will destroy all your places of worship and incense altars;
- your cities will be ruined;
- I will refuse to accept your sacrifices;
- I will destroy your land
- I will scatter you into foreign lands
- You will die in exile

God used his favorite number to increase the people's punishment!
[1] This story comes from Leviticus Chapter 26

Miriam [1]

Miriam was Aaron's wife.
Aaron was Moses' brother and a Levite....

Moses had married a Cushite (Sudanese) woman. Aaron and his wife Miriam had criticized him for it. They said,

"Has the Lord only spoken to Moses?" "Hasn't he spoken to us?"

The Lord had heard what they said.

(Moses was the most humble person on earth)

The Lord called the three of them to the Tent of his Presence.

The Lord came down in a pillar of cloud and stood at the entrance of the Tent. He said,

"Aaron, Miriam. Now hear what I have to say.

When there are prophets amongst you, I reveal myself to them in visions and speak to them in dreams. It is
    different when I speak to my servant Moses. I have put him in charge of my people Israel.
"Jesus was faithful to God, who chose him to do this work,
    just as Moses was faithful in his work in God's house."
(Hebrews 3:2)

So I speak to him clearly and not in riddle's - face to face, he has even seen my form. How dare you speak against my servant Moses?"

The Lord was angry with them so he departed and the cloud left the Tent.

Miriam's skin was suddenly covered with the dreaded disease and turned white as snow. When Aaron saw this he said to Moses,

"Please Sir, do not make us suffer this punishment for our foolish sin. Don't let her become something born dead
with half its flesh eaten away."

So Moses called out to the Lord, "Oh God heal her."
The Lord answered,

"If her father had spat in her face, she would have had to bear her disease for _**seven**_ days. So let her be shut out
of the camp for _**seven**_ days and after that she can be brought back in!"

Miriam was shut out of the camp for _**seven**_ days and the people did not move on until she was brought back in.

[1] This story comes from Numbers Chapter 12

<u>Balaam</u> [1]

Balaam was a prophet and lived near the River Euphrates....

King Balak, of Moab, sent messengers to summon Balaam,
son of Beor. They brought Balaam this message from Balak,

"I want you to know that a whole nation has come from Egypt; its
people are spreading everywhere and
threatening to take over our land. They outnumber us, so please
come and put a curse on them for me. Then
perhaps we will be able to defeat them and drive them out of the
land. I know that when you pronounce a
blessing, people are blessed, and when you pronounce a curse, they
are placed under a curse."

Balaam replied,

"Spend the night here, and tomorrow I will report to you
whatever the Lord tells me."

God came to Balaam and asked,
"Who are these people staying with you?" Balaam answered,

"King Balak of Moab has sent them to tell me that I must curse the
Israelites, so he can fight them and drive them
out."

God said,

"Do not go with these men and do not put a curse on the
people of Israel, because they have my blessings."

The messengers returned to Balak and told him Balaam had refused to go with them. Balak then sent more important men to Balaam.

Balak's message said,

"Please do not let anything prevent you from coming to me. I will reward you richly. Please come and curse the
people for me."

Balaam answered,

"Even if Balak gives me all the silver and gold in his palace, I could not disobey the command of the Lord my
God."

That night the Lord came to Balaam and said,

"If these men have asked you to go, get ready to go, but do only what I tell you." Balaam saddled his donkey and went with them.

When he arrived, Balak asked Balaam,

"Why didn't you come when I sent for you? Did you not think I was able to reward you enough?" Balaam answered,

"I came, didn't I? But what power have I got? I can only say what God tells me what to say."

The next morning Balak took Balaam up to Bamoth Baal.

Balaam said to Balak,

"Build seven altars here for me. And bring me _**seven**_ bulls and _**seven**_ rams."

Balak did as he was told and he and Balaam offered a bull and a ram on each altar. Then Balaam said to Balak,

"Stand here by your burnt offering, while I go see whether or not the Lord will meet me. I will tell you whatever he reveals to me."

So he went alone to the top of the hill and God met him. Balaam said to him,

"I have built the _**seven**_ altars and offered a bull and a ram on each."

The Lord told Balaam what to say and he went back to Balak and all the leaders of Moab.

Balaam spoke,

"How can I curse what God has not cursed? Or speak of doom when the Lord has not?" Then Balak said to Balaam,

"What have you done to me? I brought you here to curse my enemies, but all you have done is bless them." He answered,

"I can only say what the Lord has told me to say."

Balak took Balaam to the top of Mount Pisgah, where they could see some of the Israelites. There they also built _**seven**_ altars and offered a bull and a ram on each of them.

The Lord once again told Balaam what to say. He said to Balak and the leaders,

"God is not like men, who lie;

He is not a human who changes his mind.

Whatever he promises, he does;

He speaks, and it is done.

I have been instructed to bless,

And when God blesses, I cannot call it back.

The nation of Israel is like a mighty lion,

It doesn't rest until it has torn and devoured,

Until it has drunk the blood of those it has killed."

Then Balak said to Balaam,

"You refuse to curse the people of Israel, but at least don't bless them." Balaam answered,

"Didn't I tell you that I had to do everything that the Lord told me!"

Balak took Balaam to another place, to the top of Mount Peor overlooking the desert. Balaam said to him,

"Build **_seven_** altars for me here and bring me **_seven_** bulls and **_seven_** rams." Balak did as he was told and offered a bull and a ram on each altar.

By now Balaam knew the Lord wanted him to bless the people of Israel. He turned to the desert and he saw the people of Israel camped tribe by tribe.

The spirit of God took control of him, and he uttered this prophecy:

"The message of Balaam son of Beor,

The words of a man who can see clearly,

Who can hear what God is saying,

With staring eyes I see in a trance A vision from Almighty God.

The tents of Israel are beautiful,

Like long rows of palms

Or gardens besides a river,

Like aloes planted by the Lord Or cedars besides the water.

They will have abundant rainfall

And plant their seed in well-watered fields.

Their king shall be greater than Agag,

And his rule shall be extended far and wide.

God brought them out of Egypt;

He fights for them like a wild ox.

They devour their enemies,

Crush their bones, smash their arrows.

The nation is like a mighty lion,

When it is sleeping, no one dares wake it.

Whoever blesses Israel will be blessed,

And whoever curses Israel will be cursed."

Balak clenched his fists in anger and said,

"I called you to curse my enemies, but three times now you have blessed them instead. Now go off home. I promised to reward you, but the Lord has kept you from getting any reward."

Balaam answered,

"I told the messengers you sent me, that even if you gave me all the silver and gold in your palace, I could not disobey the command of the Lord by doing anything by myself. I will only say what the Lord tells me to say.

Now I am going back to my own people, but before I go, I am warning you what the people of Israel will do to your people in the future.

"The message of Balaam son of Beor,

The words of a man who can see clearly,

Who can hear what God is saying

And receive the knowledge that comes from the Most High.

With staring eyes I see in a trance

A vision from Almighty God.

I look into the future,

And I see the nation of Israel,

A king, like a bright star, will arise in that nation,

Like a comet he will come from Israel.

He will strike the leaders of Moab And beat down all the people of Seth.

He will conquer his enemies in Edom And make their land his property,

While Israel continues victorious.

The nation of Israel will trample them down

And wipe out the last survivors."

Then Balaam got ready and went back home.

[1] This story is taken from Numbers Chapters 22-24

_____The Lord's own people [1]

The Lord your God will bring you into the land which you are going to occupy - and he will drive many nations
out of it.

As you advance he will drive out **_seven_** nations larger and more powerful than you:

- The Hittites

- The Girgashites

- The Amorites

- The Canaanites

- The Perizzites

- The Hillites

- The Jebusites

When the Lord your God places these people in your power and you defeat them, you must:

- put them all to death;

- not make an alliance with them;

- do not marry any of them and do not let your children marry them.

They will lead you and your children away from the Lord to worship other gods. If that happens the Lord will be angry with you and destroy you at once.

- He will tear down their altars;

- Break down their sacred stone pillars;

- Cut down their symbols of their goddess Asherah;

- Burn their idols.

Do this because you belong to the Lord your God.

From all the peoples on the earth he chose you to be his own special people.

> Remember that the Lord your God is the _only_ God and that he is faithful;

> He will keep his covenant;

> He will show his constant love to a thousand generations of those who love and obey him; BUT HE WILL NOT HESITATE TO PUNISH THOSE WHO HATE HIM.

"He destroyed _seven_ nations in the land of Canaan and made his people the owners of the land."
(Acts 13:19)

[1] This story comes from Deuteronomy Chapter 7

Division of the Land [1]

The Sovereign Lord said,

"I solemnly promised your ancestors that I would give them possession of this land; now divide it equally among
you.....

Divide the land among your tribes; it is to be your permanent possession. The foreigners who are living among
you and have children born here are also to receive their share of the land when you divide it. They are to be
treated like full Israelite citizens and are to draw lots for shares of the land along with the tribes of Israel.
Each foreign resident will receive his share with the people of the tribe among whom he is living, I the
Sovereign Lord have spoken.
The northern boundary of the land runs eastwards from the Mediterranean Sea to the city of Hethion to Hamath
Pass to the city of Enon, to the boundary between the kingdoms of Damascus and Hamath. Each tribe is to
receive one section of land extending from the eastern boundary westwards to the Mediterranean Sea, in the
following order from north to south:

- Dan
- Asher
- Naphtali
- Manesseh
- Ephraim
- Reuben

- Judah

Seven tribes in all.

"The land will be divided among them in *seven* parts; Judah will stay in its territory in the south, and Joseph in its territory in the north. Write down a description of these *seven* divisions and bring it to me."

(Joshua 18:5-6)

[1] This story is taken from Ezekiel Chapter 47-48

The fall of Jericho [1]

The Lord had spoken to Moses' helper, Joshua son of Nun.
He said,

"My servant Moses is dead. Get ready now, you and all the people of
Israel, and cross the River Jordan into the
   land that I am giving them."

   Joshua sent spies to explore the land of Canaan, especially
   the city of Jericho. The spies returned and told Joshua,

   "We are sure that the Lord has given us the whole country.
   All the people are terrified of us"..

   The gates of Jericho were kept shut and guarded to keep the
   Israelites out.
   Nobody could enter or leave the city. The Lord said to
   Joshua,

"I am putting into your hands, Jericho, with its king and all its brave
soldiers. You and your soldiers are to march
   round the city once a day for six days.
   Seven priests, each carrying a trumpet, are to go in front of the
Covenant Box.
   On the **_seventh_** day you and your soldiers are to march round the
city **_seven_** times while the priests blow out their
   trumpets.

   Then they are to sound out the long note.

   As soon as you hear it, all the men are to give a loud shout and the
city walls will collapse then the whole army

will go straight into the city."

Joshua did as the Lord said.

So just as Joshua had ordered, an advanced guard started out ahead of the priests who were blowing trumpets,
behind these were the priests who were carrying the Covenant Box, followed by a rearguard. All this time the
trumpets were sounding.

But Joshua had ordered the men not to shout, not to say a word until he gave the order. So he told the group of men to take the Lord's Covenant Box round the city once.

Then they came back to the camp and spent the night there. They did this for six days.

On the **_seventh_** day they got up at daybreak and marched **_seven_** times around the city in the same way.

———————————This was the only day they marched around it seven times.

The **_seventh_** time round, when the priests were about to sound the trumpets, Joshua ordered his men to shout and
said,

"The Lord has given you the city. The city and everything in it must be totally destroyed as an offering to the
Lord. Only the prostitute Rahab and her household will be spared because she hid our spies. But you are not to
take anything that is to be destroyed; if you do you will bring trouble and destruction to the Israelite camp.

Everything made of silver, gold, bronze or iron is set apart for the Lord. It is to be put in the Lord's treasury."

So the priests blew the trumpets.

As soon as the men heard it they gave a loud shout and the walls collapsed.

"It was Faith that made the walls of Jericho fall down after the Israelites had marched round them for seven
days."
(Hebrews 11:30)

Then all the army went straight up the hill into the city and captured it. With their swords they killed everyone in the city and all the animals.

They saved Rahab and her family and then set fire to the city and burnt it to the ground along with everything in it except the things for the Lord's treasury.

"It was Faith that kept the prostitute Rahab from being killed with those who disobeyed God, for she gave the Israelite spies a friendly welcome."
(Hebrews 11:31)

At that time Joshua issued a solemn warning:

"Anyone who tries to rebuild the city of Jericho will be under the Lord's curse. Whoever lays the foundation will lose his eldest son.

Whoever builds the gates will lose his youngest."

"During his reign Hiel from Bethel rebuilt Jericho. As the Lord had foretold through Joshua son of Nun, Hiel lost his eldest son Abiram when he laid the foundation of Jericho, and his youngest son Segub when he built the gates."
(1 Kings 16:34)

[1] This story is taken from Joshua chapter 6

<u>Gideon</u> [1]

There was peace in the land of Israel for forty years but.....

Once again the people of Israel sinned against the Lord, so
he let the people of Midian rule them for <u>*seven*</u>

years.
The Midianites were stronger than Israel, and the people of Israel
hid from them in caves and other safe places
in the hills.

The Midianites came and devastated the land and Israel was
helpless against them.

Then the people of Israel cried out to the Lord for help and the
Lord sent them a prophet who brought them this
message from the Lord, the God of Israel,
"I brought you out of slavery in Egypt. I rescued you from the
Egyptians and from the people who fought against
you here in this land. I drove them out as you advanced, and I gave
you the land. I told you that I am the Lord your
God and you should not worship the gods of the Amorites, whose
land you are now living in. But you did not listen
to me."
The Lord's angel came to Gideon who was threshing some wheat
secretly in a wine press, so that the
Midianites would not see him.

The Lord's angel said,
"The Lord is with you, brave and mighty man!" Gideon said
to him,

"If I may ask, Sir, why has all this happened to us if the Lord is with
us? What about all the wonderful things

that our fathers told us the Lord used to do - how he brought them out of Egypt? The Lord has abandoned us
and left us to the mercy of the Midianites."

The Lord ordered him,

"Go with all your great strength and rescue Israel from the Midianites. I myself am sending you." Gideon replied,

"But how can I rescue Israel? My tribe is the weakest in the tribe of Manassaeh, and I am the least important
member of my family."

The Lord answered,

"You can do it because I will help you. You will crush the Midianites as easily as if they were only one man." Gideon replied,

"If you are pleased with me, give me some proof that you are really the Lord. Please do not leave until I bring
you an offering of food."

The Lord said,
"I will stay with you until you come back."

So Gideon went and cooked a young goat and baked some bread and gave them to the Lord's angel. The angel ordered him,

"Put the meat and the bread on this rock, and pour the broth over them."

Then the Lord's angel reached out and touched the meat and the bread with the end of the stick he was holding.

Fire came out and burnt up the meat and the bread. Then the angel disappeared.

Gideon then realized that it was the Lord's angel he had seen, and he said in terror, "Sovereign Lord! I have seen your angel face to face."

But the Lord said to him,

"Peace. Don't be afraid. You will not die. Take your father's bull and another bull seven years old, tear down your father's altar to Baal and cut down the symbol of the goddess Asherah. Build a well-constructed altar to the Lord your God on top of this mound. Then take the second bull and burn it whole as an offering, using for fire the symbol of Asherah you have burnt down."

Gideon was too afraid of his family and the people of the town to do it by day, so he did it by night.

The next day Gideon defeated the Midianites.

The Lord even made him reduce his army so that the people would see that it was the Lord that had defeated them.

"We will take for our own the land that belongs to God."
(Psalms 83:12)

He defeated the people who had ruled them for **_seven_** years!!!!

[1] This story is taken from Judges Chapters 6-7

Samson [1]

The Israelites sinned against the Lord again, and he let the Philistines rule them for forty years....

There was a man named Manoah whose wife couldn't have children. The Lord's angel appeared to her and said,

"You have never been able to have children, but you will soon be pregnant and have a son. Take care not to

drink any wine or beer, or eat any forbidden food; and after your son is born, you must never cut his hair,

because from the day of his birth he will be dedicated to God as a Nazirite (A person who showed his devotion

to God by taking vows not to drink wine or beer or cut his hair or touch corpses - Numbers 6:1-8).

He will begin the work of rescuing Israel from the Philistines." Once the angel had left, Manoah prayed to the Lord,

"Please Lord, let the man of God that you sent come back to us and tell us what we must do with the boy when

he is born."

The Lord did as he asked and the angel came back. Manoah said to the angel,

"When your words come true, what must the boy do? What kind of life must he lead?" The angel answered,

"Your wife must be sure to do everything that I have told her."

So Manoah took a young goat and some grain, and offered them on a rock altar to the Lord who works wonders.

The woman gave birth to a son and named him Samson. The child grew and the Lord blessed him. And the Lord's power began to strengthen him.

One day Samson noticed a certain Philistine girl. He said his parents,

"There is a certain Philistine girl who has caught my attention. Get her for me. I want to marry her." His parents asked him,

"Why do you have to go to those heathen Philistines to get a wife? Can't you find a girl in your own clan, amongst all our people?"

But Samson was determined that she was the one that he liked.

His parents did not know that it was the Lord that was leading Samson to do this, for the Lord was looking for a chance to fight the Philistines.

Samson killed a lion with his bare hands. He tore the lion apart as the power of the Lord made Samson strong.

A few days later Samson went to look at the lion he had killed and was surprised to find a swarm of bees and some honey inside the dead body. He ate some of the honey and took the rest home to his parents.

Samson gave a banquet at the girl's house.

This was a custom among the young men. The Philistines sent 30 men to stay with him. Samson said to them,

"Let me ask you a riddle. I'll bet each one of you a piece of fine linen and change of fine clothes that you can't tell me the meaning before the **_seven_** days of the wedding feast are over."

They all wanted to hear the riddle so Samson said, "Out of the eater came something to eat.

Out of the strong came something sweet."

On the fourth day the Philistines said to Samson's wife,

"Trick your husband into telling us what the riddle means. If you don't, we will set fire to your father's house and burn it with you."

So Samson's wife went to Samson crying,

"You don't love me! You asked my friends a riddle but you didn't tell me what it means!" Samson said,

"I haven't even told my parents. Why should I tell you?" She cried for the whole seven days of the feast.

But he told her on the seventh day what the riddle meant because she nagged him too much. Then she told the Philistines.

The men told Samson the meaning of the riddle, "What could be sweeter than honey?

What could be stronger than a lion?" Samson replied,

"If you hadn't been plugging my cow. You wouldn't know the answer now."

Suddenly the power of the Lord made him strong and he killed 30 Philistines, stripped them and gave their fine clothes to the men who had solved the riddle.

He went home furious with what had happened and his wife was given to his best man at the wedding. Samson went and caught 300 foxes. Two by two he tied their tails together and put torches in the knots. Then he set fire to the torches and turned the foxes loose in the Philistine cornfields.

Samson had done this as his father-in-law had given Samson's wife away.

So the Philistines went and burnt the woman to death and burnt down her father's house.

But Samson took revenge and killed many of them and then went to live in a cave in the cliff at Etam. Samson led Israel for 20 years.

After a while he fell in love with a woman named Delilah.

The five Philistine kings went to her and told her to trick Samson into telling her what made him so strong.

They each offered her 1100 pieces of silver.

Delilah asked Samson,

"Please tell me what makes you so strong? If someone wants to tie you up and make you helpless, how could he do it?"

Samson answered,

"If they tie me up with _**seven**_ new bow strings that are not dried out, I will be as weak as anybody else."

So the Philistine kings brought Delilah seven new bowstrings which she tied Samson up with. But Samson snapped them so the Philistines still did not know the secret of his strength.

Delilah asked him again and this time he said she must tie him up with ropes. But when the Philistines came he snapped the ropes.

Delilah asked him again and he told her to take seven locks of his hair and weave them together into the loom.

But he woke up and pulled his hair loose from the loom.

She kept on asking him day after day until he was so sick of her nagging that he finally told her the truth, "My hair has never been cut. I have been dedicated to the Lord as a Nazirite from the time I was born. If my

hair was cut I would lose all my strength and be as weak as everyone else."

Then Delilah lulled Samson to sleep and then called a man who cut off Samson's seven locks of hair. The Lord left Samson and he lost all his strength.

The Philistines captured him and put his eyes out.

The Philistine kings gathered everyone to offer sacrifices to their god Dagon. They wanted Samson to entertain them so they tied him up between two pillars. All five kings were there and about 3000 men and women.

Then Samson prayed,

"Sovereign Lord, please remember me. Please God give me my strength once more.

So with one blow I can get even with the Philistines for putting out my two eyes."

He took hold of the two pillars and pushed against them shouting, "Let me die with the Philistines."

The building fell down killing the kings and the Philistines.

Samson killed more people at his death than he had killed during his life!

[1] This story is taken from Judges Chapters 13-16

Ruth [1]

The peaceful story of Ruth is set in the violent times of the
book of Judges.

Ruth was a Moabite woman whose Israelite husband died and she
showed uncommon loyalty to her Israelite
mother-in-law (Naomi) and deep devotion to the God of Israel.

But she found a new husband....

Boaz went to the meeting place at the town gate and sat down
there. Then Elimelech's nearest relative came by
and Boaz called to him,

"Come over here, my friend, and sit down."

So he went over and sat down.

Then Boaz got ten of the leaders of the town and asked them
to sit down there too. When they were seated he said to the
relative,

"Now that Naomi has come back from Moab, she wants to sell the
field that belonged to our relative Elimelech,
and I think you ought to know about it. Now then, if you want it,
buy it in the presence of the men sitting here.
But if you don't want it, say so, because the right to buy it belongs
first to you and then to me."

The man said, "I will buy it." Boaz said,

"Very well, but if you buy the field from Naomi, then you are also
buying Ruth, the Moabite widow, so that the

field will stay in the dead man's family."

The man answered,

"In that case I will give up my right to buy the field because it would mean that my own children would not
inherit it. You buy it; I would rather not."
Now in those days to settle a sale or an exchange of property, it was the custom for the seller to take off his sandal
and give it to the buyer. In this way the Israelites showed that the matter was settled.

So when the man said to Boaz,

"You buy it", he took off his sandal and gave it to Boaz. Then
Boaz said to the leaders,

"You are all witnesses today that I have brought from Naomi everything that belonged to Elimelech and to his
sons Chilion and Mahlon.
In addition, Ruth the Moabite, Mahlon's widow, becomes my wife. This will keep the property in the dead
man's family and his family line will continue among his people and in his town. You are witnesses to this
today."

The leaders said,

"Yes we are all witnesses! May the Lord make your wife become like Rachel and Leah, who bore many children to
Jacob. May the children that the Lord will give you by this young woman make your family like the family of
Perez, the son of Judah and Tamar,"
So Boaz took Ruth home as his wife.

The Lord blessed her and she became pregnant and had a son. All the women said to Naomi,

"Praise the Lord! He has given you a grandson today to take care of you. May the boy become famous in Israel!

Your daughter-in-law loves you, and has done more for you than **_seven_** sons. And now she has given a grandson,

who will bring new life to you and give you security in your old age."

Naomi took the child, held him close and took care of him. The women of the neighborhood named the boy Obed.

Obed became the father of Jesse, who was the father of King David. Amen.

Ruth said,

"Don't ask me to leave you! Let me go with you. Wherever you go, I will go; wherever you live, I will live. Your people will be my people, and your God will be my God. Wherever you die, I will die, and that is where I will be buried. May the Lord's worst punishment come upon me if I let anything but death separate me from you!"

(Ruth 1:16-17)

[1] This story is taken from Ruth Chapter 4

__Hannah's Prayer__ [1]

Samuel was the last of the great judges. This is the story of his birth....

The Lord had kept Hannah from having children. Penninnah, her rival, would torment and humiliate her, because

the Lord had kept her from having children.

This went on year after year; whenever they went to the house of the Lord, Penninnah would upset Hannah so

much that she would cry and refuse to eat anything.

Her husband Elkanah would ask her, "Hannah, why are you crying?
Why won't you eat?
Don't I mean more to you than ten sons?"

One day after they had finished their meal in the house of the Lord at Shiloh, Hannah got up. She was deeply

distressed, and she cried bitterly as she prayed to the Lord.

Meanwhile Eli the priest was sitting in his place by the door. Hannah made a solemn promise,

"Lord Almighty, look at me, your servant! See my trouble and remember me!

Don't forget me!

If you give me a son, I promise I will dedicate Him to you for his whole life and that he will never have his hair cut."

(A sign of dedication to the Lord)

Hannah continued to pray to the Lord for a long time and Eli watched her lips. She was praying silently; her lips were moving, but she made no sound.

So Eli thought she was drunk and said to her, "Stop making a drunken show of yourself!

Stop your drinking and sober up!" "No, I'm not drunk, Sir," she answered. "I haven't been drinking!

I am desperate, and I have been praying, pouring out my troubles to the Lord. Don't think I am a worthless woman. I have been praying like this because I am miserable."

"Go in peace," Eli said, "and may the God of Israel give you what you have asked him for." "May you always think kindly of me," she replied.

Then she went away, ate some food and was no longer sad.

The next morning Elkanah and his family got up early, and after worshipping the Lord, they went back home to Ramah.

Elkanah had intercourse with his wife Hannah, and the Lord answered her prayer. So it was that she became pregnant and gave birth to a son.

She named him Samuel and explained, "I asked the Lord for him."

(In Hebrew Samuel means "Ask God")

Hannah told her husband,

"As soon as the child is weaned, I will take him to the house of the Lord, where he will stay for all of his life."

After she had weaned him, she took him to Shiloh, taking along a three-year old bull, ten kilograms of flour and a leather bag full of wine.

After they had killed the bull, they took the child to Eli. Hannah said to him,

"Excuse me, Sir.

Do you remember me?

I am the woman you saw standing here, praying to the Lord.

I asked him for this child, and he gave me what I asked for.

So I am dedicating him to the Lord.

As long as he lives, he will belong to the Lord." Then they worshipped the Lord there.

Hannah prayed:

"The Lord has filled my heart with joy;

How happy I am because of what he has done! I laugh at my enemies;

How joyful I am because God has helped me! No one is holy like the Lord,

there is none like him,

no protector like our God.

Stop your loud boasting, silence your proud words.

For the Lord is a God who knows, and he judges all that people do.

The bows of strong soldiers are broken, but the weak grow strong.

The people who once were well fed now hire themselves out to get food, but the hungry are hungry no more.

The childless wife has borne __seven__ children, but the mother of many is left with none.

The Lord kills and restores to life;

He sends people to the world of the dead, and brings them back again.

He makes some men poor and others rich; He humbles some and makes others great He lifts the poor from the dust

and raises the needy from their misery, He makes them companions of princes and puts them in places of honour.

The foundations of earth belong to the Lord; on them he has built the world.

He protects the lives of his faithful people but the wicked disappear in darkness;

a man does not triumph by his own strength. The Lord's enemies will be destroyed;

He will thunder against them from heaven. The Lord will judge the whole world;

He will give power to his king,

He will make his chosen king victorious!"

Mary said,
"My heart praises the Lord;
My soul is glad because of God my Savior, For he has remembered me, his lowly servant! From now on all people will call me happy, Because of the great things the Mighty God has done to me. His name is Holy; From one generation to another He shows mercy to those who honor him. He has stretched out his mighty arm

*And scattered the proud with all their plans. He has brought
down mighty kings
From their thrones and lifted up the lowly. He has filled the
hungry with good things, And sent the rich away with empty
hands. He has kept the promise he made
To our ancestors,
And has come to the help of his servant Israel. He has
remembered to show mercy
To Abraham and
To all his descendants forever!"
(Luke 1:46-55)*

*The boy Samuel stayed in Shiloh and served the Lord under
the priest Eli.*
[1] *This story is taken from 1 Samuel Chapters 1-2*

Saul is acclaimed as king [1]

The leaders of Israel had met with Samuel to ask him to appoint a king to rule over them, so they could have a
king like other countries had.

Samuel prayed to the Lord and the Lord instructed Samuel
to listen to the people.....

Samuel called the people together for a religious gathering in
Mizpah and said to them, "The Lord, the God of Israel says,

'I brought you out of Egypt and rescued you from the Egyptians and all the other peoples who were oppressing
you. I am your God, the one who rescues you from all your troubles and difficulties, but today you have rejected
me and have asked me to give you a king. Very well then, gather yourselves before the Lord by tribes and by
clans.'"
Then Samuel made each tribe come forward, and the Lord picked the tribe of Benjamin. Then Samuel made the
families of the tribe of Benjamin come forward, and the family of Matri was picked out. Then the men of the
family of Matri came forward, and Saul, son of Kish was picked out. They looked for him, but when they could
not find him, they asked the Lord,

"Is there still someone else?" The Lord answered,

"Saul is over there, hiding behind the supplies."

So they ran and brought Saul out to the people and they could see that he was a head taller than anyone else. Samuel said to the people,

"Here is the man the Lord has chosen! There is no one else among us like him." All the people shouted,

"Long live the king!"

Samuel explained to the people the rights and duties of the king, and then wrote them in a book, which he deposited in a holy place. Then he sent everyone home.

Saul also went home to Gibeah.

Some powerful men whose hearts God has touched, went with him. But some worthless people said,

"How can this fellow do us any good?"

They despised Saul and did not bring him any gifts.

About a month later King Nahash of Ammon led his army against the town of Jabesh in the territory of Gilead and besieged it.

The men of Jabesh said to Nahash,

"Make a treaty with us, and we will accept you as our ruler." Nahash answered,

"I will make a treaty with you on one condition; I will put out everyone's right eye and so bring disgrace on all Israel."
The leaders of Jabesh said,

"Give us _**seven**_ days to send messengers throughout the land of Israel. If no one will help us, then we will

surrender to you."

The messengers arrived at Gibeah, where Saul lived, and when they told the news, the people started crying in

despair.

Saul was just coming in from the field with his oxen, and he asked, "What's wrong?

Why is everyone crying?"

They told him what the messengers from Jabesh had reported.

When Saul heard this, the spirit of God took control of him, and he became furious.

He took two oxen, cut them in pieces, and sent messengers to carry the pieces throughout the land of Israel

with this warning:

"Whoever does not follow Saul and Samuel into battle will have this done to his oxen!"

The people of Israel were afraid of what the Lord might do, and all of them, without exception, came out

together.

Saul gathered them at Bezek: there were 300,000 from Israel and 30,000 from Judah. They said to the

messengers from Jabesh,

"Tell your people that before noon tomorrow they will be rescued."

When the people of Jabesh received the message, they were overjoyed and said to Nahash, "Tomorrow we will

surrender to you, and you can do with us whatever you wish."

Early the next day, Saul divided his men into three groups, and at dawn they rushed into the enemy camp and

attacked the Ammonites.

By noon they had slaughtered them.

The survivors scattered, each man running off by himself.

Then the people of Israel said to Samuel,

"Where are the people who said that Saul should not be our king? Hand them over to us, and we will kill them!"

But Saul said,

"No one will be put to death today, for this is the day the Lord rescued Israel." And Samuel said to them,

"Let us all go to Gilgal and once more proclaim Saul as our king."

So they all went to Gilgal, and there at the holy place they proclaimed Saul king.

They offered fellowship-sacrifices, and Saul and all the people of Israel celebrated the event!

[1] This story is taken from 1 Samuel Chapter 10&11

The death of Saul and his sons [1]

"Saul died because he was unfaithful to the Lord. He disobeyed the Lord's commands; he tried to find guidance by consulting the spirits of the dead instead of consulting the Lord....."
(1 Chronicles 10:13)

The Philistines fought a battle against the Israelites on Mount Gilboa.

Many Israelites were killed there, and the rest of them, including King Saul and his sons, fled.

But the Philistines caught up with them and killed three of Saul's sons, Jonathan, Abinadab and Malchishua.

The fighting was heavy round Saul, and he himself was hit by enemy arrows and badly wounded.

He said to the young man carrying his weapons,

"Draw your sword and kill me, so that these godless Philistines won't gloat over me and kill me." But the young man was too terrified to do it.

So Saul took his own sword and threw himself on it.

The young man saw that Saul was dead, so he too threw himself on his own sword and died with Saul. And that is how Saul, his three sons and the young man died; all of Saul's men died that day.

When the Israelites on the other side of the valley of Jezreel and east of the river Jordan heard that the Israelite

army had fled and that Saul and his sons had been killed, they abandoned their towns and fled.

Then the Philistines came and occupied them.

The day after the battle the Philistines went to plunder the corpses, and they found the bodies of Saul and his

three sons lying on Mount Gilboa.

They cut off Saul's head, stripped off his armour, and sent messengers with them throughout Philistia to tell

the good news to their idols and to their people.

Then they put Saul's weapons in the temple of the goddess Astarte, and they nailed his body to the wall of the city

of Beth Shan.

When the people of Jabesh in Gilead heard what the Philistines had done to Saul, the bravest men started out

and marched all night to Beth Shan. They took down the bodies of Saul and his sons from the wall, brought

them back to Jabesh, and burnt them there.

Then they took the bones and buried them under a tamarisk-tree in the town, and fasted for _**seven**_ days!

[1] This story is taken from 1 Samuel Chapter 31

David [1]

Samuel was sent by the Lord to Bethlehem, to a man named
Jesse, to anoint one of his sons king. Jesse brought **_seven_** of
his sons to Samuel but the Lord had not chosen any of them.

Jesse sent for his youngest son David, who was out taking care of the
sheep, and David was anointed king in front
of his **_seven_** brothers....

During David's reign there was a severe famine which lasted
for three full years. So David consulted the Lord about it,
and the Lord said,

"Saul and his family are guilty of murder; he put the people
of Gideon to death."

(The people of Gideon were not Israelites; they were a small group
of Amorites whom the Israelites had promised
to protect, but Saul had tried to destroy them because of his zeal for
the people of Israel and Judah).

So David summoned the people of Gideon and said to them,
"What can I do for you?

I want to make up for the wrong that was done to you, so
that you will bless the Lord's people." They answered,

"Our quarrel with Saul and his family can't be settled with silver or
gold, nor do we want to kill any Israelite."

"What, then, do you think I should do for you?" David
asked.

They answered,

"Saul wanted to destroy us and leave none of us alive anywhere in Israel. So hand over **_seven_** of his male

descendants, and we will hang them before the Lord at Gibeah, the town of Saul, the Lord's chosen king."

"I will hand them over," King David replied.

But because of the sacred promise that he and Jonathan had made to each other, David spared Jonathan's son

Mephibosheth, the grandson of Saul. However he took Armoni and Mephibosheth, the two sons that Rizpah the

daughter of Aiah had borne to Saul; he also took the five sons of Saul's daughter Merab, whom she had borne to

Adriel son of Barzillai, who was from Meholah.

David handed them over to the people of Gibeon, who hanged them on the mountain before the Lord — and all

seven of them died together.

It was late in the spring, at the beginning of the barley harvest, when they were put to death.

Then Saul's concubine Rizpah, the daughter of Aiah, used sackcloth to make a shelter for herself on the rock

where the corpses were, and she stayed there from the beginning of the harvest until the autumn rains came.

During the day she would keep the birds away from the corpses, and at night she would protect them from wild

animals.

When David had heard what Rizpah had done, he went and got the bones of Saul and of his son Jonathan from

the people of Jabesh in Gilead.

(They had stolen them from the public square in Beth Shan, where the Philistines had hanged the bodies on the
day they killed Saul on Mount Gilboa).
David took the bones of Saul and Jonathan and also gathered up the bones of the **_seven_** men who had been
hanged.
Then they buried the bones of Saul and Jonathan in the grave of Saul's father Kish, in Zela in the territory of
Benjamin, doing all that the king had commanded.
And after that, God answered their prayers for the country.

"The promises of the Lord can be trusted;
They are as genuine as silver refined _seven_ times in the furnace."
Psalm 12:6 (A Psalm by David)

[1] This story is taken from 2 Samuel Chapter 16 & 31

King Solomon's wealth [1]

King David said to his priest, a prophet and his bodyguard,

"Take my court officials with you; let my son Solomon ride my own mule and escort him down to the springs of
Gihon, where Solomon is to be anointed king of Israel. Follow him back here when he comes to sit on my throne.
He will succeed me as king, because he is the one I have chosen to be the ruler of Israel and Judah."...

Solomon made an alliance with the king of Egypt by marrying his daughter.

He brought her to live in David's City until he had finished building his palace, the Temple and the wall around
Jerusalem.

One night the Lord appeared to him in a dream and asked him, "What would you like me to give you?"

Solomon answered,

"You always showed great love for my father David, your servant, and he was good, loyal and honest in his
relations with you. And you have continued to show him your great and constant love by giving him a son today
who rules in his place. Oh Lord, God, you have let me succeed my father as king, even though I am very young
and don't know how to rule. Here I am among the people you have chosen to be your own, a people who are so
many that they cannot be counted. So give me the wisdom I need to rule your people with justice and to know

the difference between good and evil. Otherwise how will I be able to rule these great people of yours?"

The Lord was pleased that Solomon had asked for this and so he said to him,

"Because you have asked for the wisdom to rule justly, instead of long life for yourself or riches or the death of

your enemies. I will do what you have asked. I will give you more wisdom and understanding than anyone has

ever had before or will ever have again. I will also give you what you have not asked for : all your life you will

have wealth and honor, more than that of any other king. And if you obey me and keep my laws and

commands, as your father David did, I will give you a long life."

God gave Solomon unusual wisdom and insight, and knowledge too great to be measured. Solomon was wiser

than the wise men of the East or the wise men of Egypt.

He composed three thousand proverbs and more than a thousand songs.

He spoke of trees and plants; he talked about animals, birds, reptiles and fish. Kings all over the world heard of

his wisdom and they sent people to listen to him.

Every year King Solomon received almost twenty three thousand kilograms of gold in addition to the taxes paid

by the merchants, the profits from trade, and tribute paid by the Arabian kings and the governors of the

Israelite districts.

Solomon made two hundred large shields, and had each one overlaid with almost _**seven**_ kilograms of gold.

He also made three hundred smaller shields, overlaying them with gold.

He had all of these shields placed in the Hall of the Forest of Lebanon (A large ceremonial hall in the palace,

probably so called because it was paneled in cedar).

Solomon was richer and wiser than any other king and the whole world wanted to come and listen to the wisdom

that God had given him.

Solomon was king in Jerusalem over all Israel for forty years.

[1] This story is taken from 1 Kings Chapters 1-3

King Zimri [1]

When Elah was king of Israel, Zimri, one of his officers in charge of the chariots, plotted against him. One day

when Elah was getting drunk in his home, Zimri entered the house and assassinated him.....

In the ***twenty-seventh*** year of the reign of King Asa of Judah, Zimri ruled in Tirzah over Israel for ***seven*** days. As

soon as Zimri became king he killed off all the members of Baasha's family.

Every male relative and friend was put to death.

And so, in accordance with what the Lord had said against Baasha through the prophet Jehu, Zimri killed all the

family of Baasha.

Because of their idolatry and because they had led Israel into sin, Baasha and his son Elah had aroused the

anger of the Lord, the God of Israel.

The Israelite troops were besieging the city of Gibbethon in Philistia, and when they heard that Zimri had plotted

against the king and assassinated him, then and there they all proclaimed their commander Omri king of Israel.

Omri and all his troops left Gibbethon and went and besieged Tirzah.

When Zimri saw that the city had fallen, he went into the palace's inner fortress, set the palace on fire, and died

in the flames.

This happened because of his sins against the Lord.

Like his predecessor Jeroboam he displeased the Lord by his own sins and by leading Israel into sin.

[1] This story is taken from 1 Kings Chapter 16

Elijah [1]

A prophet named Elijah from Tishbe in Gilead, said to King Ahab,

"In the name of the Lord, the living God of Israel, whom I serve, I tell you that there will be no rain or dew for
the next two or three years until I say so."
"Elijah was the same kind of person as we are. He prayed earnestly that there would be no rain, and no rain fell on the land for three and a half years."
(James 5:17)

Then the Lord said to Elijah,

"Leave this place and go east and hide yourself near the brook of Cherith, east of the Jordan. The brook will

supply you with water to drink, and I have commanded ravens to bring you food there."

Elijah obeyed the Lord's command, and went and stayed by the brook of Cherith.

He drank water by the brook, and ravens brought him bread and meat every morning and every evening. After a while the brook dried up because of the lack of rain.

Then the Lord said to Elijah,

"Now go to the town of Zarephath, near Sidon, and stay there. I have commanded a widow who lives there to

feed you."

The widow provided food and water for Elijah and when her son died Elijah prayed to the Lord, "O Lord my God, restore this child to life!"

The Lord answered Elijah's prayer; the child started breathing again and revived.

After some time, in the third year of the drought, the Lord said to Elijah,

"Go and present yourself to King Ahab, and I will send rain."

Obadiah (a devout worshipper of the Lord) met Elijah on the way. Elijah said to him,

"Go and tell your master the king that I am here." Obadiah answered,

"What have I done that you want to put me in danger of being killed by King Ahab? By the living Lord, your God,

I swear that the king has made a search for you in every country in the world. And now you want me to go and

tell him that you are here? What if the spirit of the Lord carries you off to some unknown place as soon as I

leave? Then when I tell Ahab that you are here, and he can't find you, he will put me to death."

Elijah answered,

"By the Lord Almighty, whom I serve, I promise that I will present myself to the king today." So Obadiah went to get the king.

When Ahab saw Elijah he said,

"So there you are — the worst troublemaker in Israel!" Elijah replied,

"I am not the troublemaker. You are — you and your father. You are disobeying the Lord's commands and worshipping the idols of Baal".

So Elijah ordered the king to summon all the Israelites and prophets of Baal to meet at Mount Carmel. There Elijah challenged the prophets of Baal.

He challenged them to ask Baal to send fire to set wood alight and he prayed to the Lord to do the same.

The prophets of Baal prayed and prayed until the middle of the afternoon; but no answer came and not a sound was heard.

Elijah then got the people to dig a trench around the altar, large enough to hold almost fourteen litres of water.

Elijah approached the altar and prayed,

"Oh Lord, the God of Abraham, Isaac, and Jacob, prove now that you are the God of Israel and that I am your servant and have done this all at your command. Answer me, Lord, answer me, so that these people will know that you, the Lord, are God, and that you are bringing them back to yourself."

So the Lord sent fire down, and it burnt up the sacrifice, the wood and the stones, scorched the earth and dried up the water in the trench.

When the people saw this, they threw themselves on the ground and exclaimed, "The Lord is God; the Lord alone is God!"

Elijah ordered,

"Seize the prophets of Baal; don't let any of them get away!"

The people seized them all, and Elijah led them down to the River Kishon and killed them.

Then Elijah said to King Ahab,

"Now, go and eat. I hear the roaring of rain approaching."

While Ahab went to eat, Elijah climbed to the top of Mount Carmel, where he bowed down to the ground, with his head between his knees.

He said to his servant,

"Go and look towards the sea."

The servant went and returned, saying, "I didn't see anything."

**Seven** times in all Elijah told him to go and look. The _**seventh**_ time he returned and said,

"I saw a little cloud no bigger than a man's hand coming up from the sea." Elijah ordered the servant,

"Go to King Ahab and tell him to get into his chariot and go back home before the rain stops him."

In a little while the sky was covered with dark clouds, the wind began to blow and heavy rain began to fall.

"Once again Elijah prayed and the sky poured out its rain and the earth produced its crops."
(James 5:18)

Ahab got into his chariot and started back to Jezreel.

The power of the Lord came on Elijah; he fastened his clothes tight around his waist and ran ahead of Ahab all the way to Jezreel!

[1] This story is taken from 1 Kings Chapter 17-18

__War with Syria__ [1]

The Lord said to Elijah,

"Return to the wilderness near Damascus, then enter the city and anoint Hazael as king of Syria;

anoint Jehu son of Nimshi as king of Israel and anoint Elisha son of Shaphat from Abel Meholah to succeed you
   as prophet. Anyone who escapes being put to death by Hazael will be killed by Jehu, and anyone who escapes
   Jehu will be killed by Elisha. Yet I will leave __seven__ thousand people alive in Israel — all those who are loyal to
   me and have not bowed down to Baal or kissed his idol."

Elijah left and found Elisha who went and followed Elijah as his helper.

King Benhadad of Syria gathered all his troops, and supported by thirty two other rulers with their horses and
   chariots, he marched up and laid siege to Samaria, and launched attacks against it.

He sent messengers into the city of Israel to say,

"King Benhadad demands that you surrender to him your silver and gold, your women and the strongest of
   your children."

"Tell my lord, King Benhadad, that I agree; he can have me and everything I own," Ahab answered. Later the messengers came back to Ahab with another demand from Benhadad:

"I sent you word that you were to hand over all your silver and gold, your women and your children. Now,
however, I will send my officers to search your palace and the homes of your officials, and they will take
everything they consider valuable. They will be there about this time tomorrow."

King Ahab called in the leaders of the country and said,

"You see that this man wants to ruin us. He sent me a message demanding my wives and children, my silver and
gold, and I agreed."

The leaders and the people answered,

"Don't pay any attention to him; don't give in." So Ahab replied to Benhadad's messengers,

"Tell my lord my king that I agreed to his first demand, but I cannot agree to the second." The messengers left and then returned with another message,

"I will bring enough men to destroy this city of yours and carry off the rubble in their hands; may the gods strike
me dead if I don't!"

King Ahab answered,

"Tell King Benhadad that a real soldier does his boasting after battle, not before it."

Benhadad received Ahab's answer as he and his allies, the other rulers, were drinking in their tents. He ordered
his men to get ready to attack the city, so they moved into position.

Meanwhile a prophet went to King Ahab and said,

"The Lord says. 'Don't be afraid of that huge army! I will give you victory over it today, and you will know that I
am the Lord!'"

"Who will lead the attack?" Ahab asked.

The prophet answered,

"The Lord says that the young soldiers under the command of the district governors are to do it." "Who will command the main force?" Asked the king.

"You," the prophet answered.

So the king called out the young soldiers who were under the district commanders, 232 in all. Then he called out the Israelite army, a total of _seven_ thousand men.

The attack began at noon, as Benhadad and his allies were getting drunk in their tents. The young soldiers advanced first.

Scouts sent out by Benhadad reported to him that a group of soldiers were coming out of Samaria. He ordered,

"Take them alive, no matter whether they are coming to fight or to ask for peace."

The young soldiers led the attack followed by the Israelite army and each one killed the man he fought. The Syrians fled, with the Israelites in hot pursuit, but Benhadad escaped on horseback, accompanied by some of his cavalry.

King Ahab took to the field, captured the horses and chariots, and inflicted a severe defeat on the Syrians.

Then the prophet went to King Ahab and said,

"Go back and build up your forces, and make careful plans, because the king of Syria will attack again next spring."

King Benhadad's officials said to him,

"The gods of Israel are mountain gods, and that is why the Israelites defeated us. But we will certainly defeat them if we fight them in the plains. Now, remove the 32 rulers from their commands, and replace them with field commanders. Then call up an army as large as the one that deserted you, with the same number of horses and chariots. We will fight them in the plains and this time we will defeat them."

King Benhadad agreed and followed their advice.

The following spring he called up his men and marched with them to the city of Aphek to attack the Israelites.

The Israelites were called up and equipped; they marched out and camped in two groups facing the Syrians.

The Israelites looked like two small flocks of goats compared with the Syrians, who spread out over the countryside.

A prophet went to King Ahab and said, "This is what the Lord says:

"Because the Syrians say that I am a God of the hills, and not of the plains, I will give you victory over their huge army, and you and your people will know that I am the Lord."

For seven days the Syrians and the Israelites stayed in their camp, facing each other. On the seventh day they started fighting, and the Israelites killed a hundred thousand Syrians.

The survivors fled into the city of Aphek, where the city walls fell on twenty seven thousand of them.

[1] This story is taken from 1 Kings Chapter 19-20

Moab [1]

In the eighteenth year of the reign of King Jehoshaphat of Judah, Joram son of Ahab became king of Israel, and
he ruled in Samaria for twelve years.

He sinned against the Lord, but he was not as bad as his father or his mother Jezebel; he pulled down the image
his father had made for the worship of Baal.

Yet, like King Jeroboam son of Nebat before him, he led Israel into sin, and would not stop.

King Mesha of Moab bred sheep, and every year he gave as a tribute to the king of Israel 100,000 lambs, and the
wool from 100,000 sheep.

But when King Ahab of Israel died, King Mesha rebelled against Israel. At once King Joram left Samaria and gathered all his troops.

He sent word to King Jehoshaphat of Judah,

"The king of Moab has rebelled against me; will you join me in war against him?"

"I will," King Jehoshaphat replied. "I am at your disposal, and so are my men and my horses. What route
should we take for the attack?"

"We will go the long way, through the wilderness of Edom." Joram answered. So King Joram and the kings of Judah and Edom set out.

After marching for **_seven_** days they ran out of water, and there was none left for the men or the pack animals.

"We are done for!" King Joram exclaimed.

King Jehoshaphat asked,

"Is there a prophet here through whom we can consult the Lord?" An officer of King Joram's forces answered,

"Elisha son of Shaphat is here. He was Elijah's assistant." "He is a true prophet." King Jehoshaphat said.

So the three kings went to Elisha.

"Why should I help you?" Elisha said to the king of Israel. "Go and consult those prophets that your father and
mother consulted."

"No!" Joram replied."It is the Lord that put us three kings at the mercy of the king of Moab." Elisha answered,

"By the living Lord, whom I serve, I swear that I would have nothing to do with you if I didn't respect your

ally King Jehoshaphat of Judah. Now get me a musician."

As the musician played his harp, the power of the Lord came on Elisha and he said, "This is what the Lord says:
'Dig ditches all over this dry stream bed. Even though you will not see any rain or wind, this stream bed will be
filled with water, and you, your cattle, and your pack animals will have plenty to drink.'"

And Elisha continued,

"But this is an easy thing for the Lord to do; he will also give you victory over the Moabites. You will conquer all

their beautiful fortified cities; you will cut down all their fruit trees, stop all their springs, and ruin all their fertile

fields by covering them with stones."

The next morning, at the time of regular morning exercise, water came flowing from the direction of Edom, and

covered the ground.

When the Moabites heard that the three kings had come to attack them, all the men who could bear arms, from

the oldest to the youngest, were called out and stationed at the border.

When they got up the following morning, the sun was shining on the water, making it look red as blood. "It's

blood!"

They exclaimed.

"The three enemy armies must have fought and killed each other! Let's go and loot their camp!" But when they

reached the camp the Israelites attacked them and drove them back.

The Israelites kept up the pursuit, slaughtering the Moabites and destroying their cities.

As they passed a fertile field, every Israelite would throw a stone on it until finally all the fields were covered;

they also stopped up the springs and cut down the fruit trees. At last only the capital city of Kir Heres was left,

and the slingers surrounded it and attacked it.

When the king of Moab realized he was losing the battle, he took seven hundred swordsmen with him and tried

. to force his way through the enemy lines and escape to the king of Syria but he failed. So he took his eldest son, who was to succeed him as king, and offered him on the city wall as sacrifice to the god of Moab.

The Israelites were terrified (either because of what Chemosh, the god of the Moabites, might do, or because of

what the Lord, the God of the Israelites might do) and so they withdrew from the city and returned to their own

country.

[1] This story is taken from 2 Kings Chapter 3

Elisha [1]

One day Elisha went to Shunem, where a rich woman lived. She invited him to a meal, and from then on every
time he went to Shunem he would have his meals at her house.

She said to her husband,

"I am sure that this man who comes here so often is a holy man. Let's build a small room on the roof, put a bed,
a table, a chair, and a lamp on it, and he can stay there whenever he visits us."

One day Elisha returned to Shunem and went up to his room to rest. He told his servant Gehazi to go and call the woman.

When she came, he said to Gehazi,

"Ask her what I can do for her in return for all the trouble she has had for providing for our needs. Maybe she
would like me to go to the king or the army commander and put in a good word for her."

"I have all I need here among my own people," she answered. Elisha asked Gehazi,

"What can I do for her then?" He answered,

"Well, she has no son, and her husband is an old man." "Tell her to come here," Elisha ordered.

She came and stood in the doorway, and Elisha said to her,

"By this time next year you will be holding a son in your arms."

"Oh!" She exclaimed. "Please Sir, don't lie to me. You are a man of God."

But, as Elisha had said, at about that time the following year, she gave birth to a son.

"Is anything too hard for the Lord? As I said, nine months from now I will return, and Sarah will have a son."
(Genesis 18:14)

Some years later, at harvest time, the boy went out one morning to join his father, who was in the field with the harvest workers.

Suddenly he cried out to his father, "My head hurts! My head hurts!"

"Carry the boy to his mother," the father said to his servant.

The servant carried the boy back to his mother, who held him in her lap until noon, at which time he died. She carried him up to Elisha's room, put him on the bed and left, closing the door behind her.

Then she called her husband and said to him,

"Send a servant here with a donkey. I need to go to the prophet Elisha. I'll be back as soon as I can." "Why do you have to go today?" Her husband asked. "It's neither a Sabbath or a New Moon Festival." "Never mind," she answered.

Then she had the donkey saddled, and ordered the servant,

"Make the donkey go as fast as it can, and don't slow down unless I tell you to." So she set out, and went to Mount Carmel, where Elisha was.

Elisha saw her coming while she was still some distance away, and said to his servant Gehazi,

"Look — there comes the woman from Shunem! Hurry to her and find out if everything is alright with her, her husband and her son."

She told Gehazi that everything was alright, but when she came to Elisha she bowed down before him and took hold of his feet.

Gehazi was about to push her away, but Elisha said,

"Leave her alone. Can't you see that she is deeply distressed? And the Lord has not told me a thing about it." The woman said to him,

"Sir, did I ask you for a son? Didn't I tell you not to raise my hopes?" Elisha turned to Gehazi and said,

"Hurry! Take my stick and go. Don't stop to greet anyone you meet, and if anyone greets you, don't take time to answer. Go straight to the house, and hold my stick over the boy."

The woman said to Elisha,

"I swear by my loyalty to the living Lord and to you that I will not leave you!" So the two of them started back together.

Gehazi went on ahead and held Elisha's stick over the child, but there was no sound or any other sign of life. So he went back to meet Elisha and said,

"The boy didn't wake up."

When Elisha arrived, he went alone into the room and saw the boy lying dead on the bed. He closed the door and prayed to the Lord.

Then he laid down on the boy, placing his mouth, eyes and hands on the boy's mouth, eyes and hands. As he laid stretched out over the boy, the boy's body started to get warm.

Elisha got up, walked about the room, and then went back and again stretched himself over the boy. The boy sneezed **_seven_** times, and then opened his eyes.

Elisha called Gehazi and told him to call the boy's mother. When she came in, he said to her,

"Here is your son!"

She fell at Elisha's feet, with her face touching the ground. Then she took her son and left.

[1] This story is taken from 2 Kings Chapter 4

Naaman [1]

Naaman, the commander of the Syrian army, was highly respected and esteemed by the king of Syria, because

through Naaman the Lord had given victory to the Syrian forces.

He was a great soldier; but he suffered from a dreaded skin-disease.

In one of their raids against Israel, the Syrians had carried off a little Israelite girl, who became a servant of

Naaman's wife.

One day she said to her mistress,

"I wish that my master could go to the prophet who lives in Samaria! He would cure him of his disease." When Naaman heard of this, he went to the king and told him what the girl had said.

The King said,

"Go to the king of Israel and take this letter to him."

So Naaman set out, taking 30000 pieces of silver, 6000 pieces of gold and 10 changes of fine clothes. The letter that he took read:

"This letter will introduce my officer Naaman. I want you to cure him of his disease." When the king of Israel read the letter, he tore his clothes in dismay and exclaimed,

"How can the king of Syria expect me to cure this man? Does he think that I am God, with the power of life and death? It's plain that he is trying to start a quarrel with me!"

When the prophet Elisha heard what had happened, he sent word to the king:

"Why are you so upset? Send the man to me and I will show him that there is a prophet in Israel!"

So Naaman went with his horses and chariot, and stopped at the entrance to Elisha's house. Elisha sent a
servant out to tell Naaman to go wash himself **_seven_** times in the River Jordan, and he would be completely
cured of his disease.

But Naaman left in a rage saying,

"I thought that he would at least come out to me, pray to the Lord the God, wave his hand over the diseased
spot, and cure me! Besides, aren't the rivers Abana and Pharpar, back in Damascus, better than any river in
Israel? I could have washed them and been cured!"

His servants went up to him and said,

"Sir, if the prophet had told you to do something difficult, you would have done it. Now why can't you just wash
yourself, as he said, and be cured?"
So Naaman went down to the Jordan, dipped himself in it **_seven_** times, as Elisha had instructed, and he was
completely cured.

His flesh became firm and healthy like that of a child.

"And there were many people suffering from a dreaded skin-disease who lived in Israel during the time of the prophet Elisha; yet not one of them was healed, but only Naaman the Syrian"
(Luke 4:27)

He returned to Elisha with all his men and said,

"Now I know that there is no god but the God of Israel, so please, sir, accept a gift from me." Elisha answered,

"By the living Lord, whom I serve, I swear that I will not accept a gift." Naaman insisted that he accept it, but he would not.

So Naaman said,

"If you won't accept my gift, then let me have two mule-loads of earth to take home with me (It was believed that a god could be worshipped only on his own land), because from now on I will not offer sacrifices or burnt- offerings to any God except the Lord. So I hope that the Lord will forgive me when I accompany my king to the temple of Rimmon, the god of Syria, and worship him. Surely the Lord will forgive me!"

"Go in peace," Elisha said. And Naaman left.

He had gone only a short distance, when Elisha's servant, Gehazi, said to himself,

"My master had let Naaman get away without paying a thing! He should have accepted what the Syrian offered him. By the living Lord, I will run after him and get something from him."

So he set off after Naaman.

When Naaman saw a man running after him, he got down from his chariot to meet him, and asked, "Is something wrong?"

"No," Gehazi answered, "But, my master sent me to tell you that just now two members of the group of prophets in the hill-country of Ephraim arrived, and he would like you to give them 3000 pieces of silver and two changes of fine clothes."

"Please take 6000 pieces of silver," Naaman replied. He insisted on it, tied up the silver in two bags, gave them and the two changes of fine clothes to two of his servants, and sent them ahead of Gehazi.

When they reached the hill where Elisha lived, Gehazi took the two bags and carried them into the house.

Then he sent Naaman's servants back. He went back into the house and Elisha asked him, "Where have you been?"

"Oh, nowhere Sir," he answered. But Elisha said,

"Wasn't I there in spirit when the man got out of his chariot to meet you? This is no time to accept money and clothes, olive groves and vineyards, sheep and cattle, or servants! And now Naaman's disease will come upon you, and you and your descendants will have it forever."

When Gehazi left, he had the disease — his skin was as white as snow!!!

[1] This story is taken from 2 Kings Chapter 4

The Woman from Shunem returns [1]

Now Elisha told the woman who lived in Shunem, whose son he had brought back to life, that the Lord was

sending a famine on the land, which would last for ***seven*** years, and that she should leave with her family and go

and live somewhere else.

She had followed his instructions, and had gone with her family to live in Philistia for the ***seven*** years.

At the end of the ***seven*** years, she returned to Israel and went to the king to ask for her house and her land to be

returned to her.

She found the king talking with Gehazi, Elisha's servant; the king wanted to know about Elisha's miracles.

While Gehazi was telling the king how Elisha had brought a dead person back to life, the woman made her

appeal to the king.

Gehazi said to him,

"Your Majesty, here is the woman and here is her son whom Elisha brought back to life!"

In answer to the king's question, she confirmed Gehazi's story, and so the king called an official and told him to give back everything that was hers, including the value of all the crops that her field had produced during the ***seven*** years she had been away.

.[1] This story is taken from 2 Kings Chapter 8

Queen Athaliah [1]

In the twelfth year of the reign of Joram son of Ahab as king of Israel, Ahaziah son of Jehoram became king of
Judah at the age of twenty two, and he ruled in Jerusalem for one year.

His mother was Athaliah, the daughter of King Ahab and granddaughter of King Omri of Israel.

Since Ahaziah was related to King Ahab by marriage, he sinned against the Lord, just as Ahab's family did. King Ahaziah joined King Joram of Israel in a war against King Hazael of Syria.

Meanwhile the Lord had anointed Jehu king of Israel.

Jehu drew his bow, and with all his strength shot an arrow that struck Joram in the back and pierced his heart. Joram fell dead in his chariot.

King Ahaziah saw what happened, so he fled in his chariot towards the town of Beth Haggan, pursued by Jehu.

"Kill him too!" Jehu ordered his men, and they wounded him as he drove his chariot on the road up to Gur. But he managed to keep going until he reached the city of Megiddo, where he died.

His officials took his body back to Jerusalem in a chariot and buried him in the royal tombs in David's city.

As soon as King Ahaziah's mother Athaliah learnt of her son's murder, she gave an order for all the members of
the royal family to be killed.

Only Ahaziah's son Joash escaped.

He was about to be killed with the others, but he was rescued by his aunt, Jehosheba, who was King Jehoram's
daughter and Ahaziah's half sister.
She took him and his nurse into a bedroom in the Temple and hid him from Athaliah so that he was not killed.
For six years Jehosheba took care of the boy and kept him hidden in the Temple, while Athaliah ruled as queen.
But in the **_seventh_** year Jehoiada, the priest, sent for the officers in charge of the royal bodyguard and of the
palace guards, and told them to come to the Temple, where he made them agree under oath to what he
planned to do.

He showed them King Ahaziah's son
Joash and gave them the following
orders:

"When you come on duty on the Sabbath, one third of you are to guard the palace; another third are to stand
guard at the Sur Gate and the other third are to stand guard at the gate behind the other guards. The two groups
that go off duty on the Sabbath are to stand guard at the Temple to protect the king. You are to guard King Joash

with drawn swords and stay with him wherever he goes. Anyone who comes near you is to be killed."

The officers obeyed Jehoiada's instructions and brought their men to him — those going off duty on the

Sabbath and those going on duty. He gave the officers the spears and shields that had belonged to King David

and had been kept in the Temple and he stationed the men with drawn swords all round the front of the

Temple, to protect the king.

Then Jehoiada led Joash out, placed the crown on his head, and gave him a copy of the laws governing kingship.

Then Joash was anointed and proclaimed king.

The people clapped their hands and shouted, "Long live the king!"

Queen Athaliah heard the noise being made by the guards and the people, so she hurried to the Temple, where the crowd had gathered.

There she saw the new king standing by the column at the entrance of the Temple, as was the custom.

"He stood by the royal column and made a covenant with the Lord to obey him, to keep his laws and commands with all his heart and soul, and to put into practice the demands attached to the covenant as written in the book. And all the people promised to keep the covenant"
(2 Kings 23:3)

He was surrounded by the officers and the trumpeters, and the people were all shouting joyfully and blowing trumpets.

Athaliah tore her clothes in distress and shouted, "Treason! Treason!"

Jehoiada did not want Ataliah killed in the Temple area, so he ordered the army officers: "Take her out between the rows of guards, and kill anyone who tries to rescue her."

They seized her, took her to the palace, and there at the Horse Gate, they killed her.

[1] This story is taken from 2 Kings Chapter 8 & 11

The Covenant Box [1]

For his own use, David built houses in David's City.

He also prepared a place for God's Covenant Box and put a tent up for it. David said,

"Only Levites should carry the Covenant Box, because they are the ones the Lord chose to carry it and to serve
him forever."

He said to the Levites,

"You are the leaders of the Levite clans. Purify yourselves and your fellow-Levites, so that you can bring the
Covenant Box of the Lord God of Israel to the place I have prepared for it. Because you were not there to carry it
for the first time, the Lord our God punished us for not worshipping him as we should have done."
The Levites carried the Covenant Box on poles on their shoulders, as the Lord had commanded through Moses.
So King David, the leaders of Israel and the military commanders went to the house of Obed Edom to fetch the
Covenant Box, and they had a great celebration.
They sacrificed **_seven_** bulls and **_seven_** sheep, to make sure that God would help the Levites who were carrying
the Covenant Box.
David was wearing a robe made of the finest linen, and so were the musicians, Chenaniah their leader, and
the Levites who carried the Box.

David also wore an ephod.

So all the Israelites accompanied the Covenant Box up to Jerusalem with shouts of joy, the sounds of trumpets,

horns and cymbals, and the music of harps.

As the Box was being brought into the city, Michal, Saul's daughter, looked out of the window and saw King David

dancing and leaping for joy, and she was disgusted with him.

They took the Covenant Box to the tent which David had prepared for it and put it inside. Then they offered sacrifices and fellowship-offerings to God.

After David had finished offering the sacrifices, he blessed the people in the name of the Lord and distributed

food to them all.

He gave each man and woman in Israel a loaf of bread, a piece of roasted meat and some raisins.

David sang,
"Give thanks to the Lord, Because he is good;
His love is eternal.
Say to him,'Save us, O God our savior;
Gather us together, rescue us from the nations;
So that we may be thankful and praise your Holy name.'
Praise the Lord, the God of Israel.
Praise him now and forever."

Then the people all said "Amen" and praised the Lord.
[1] This story is taken from 1 Chronicles Chapter 15

Ezra [1]

When Artaxerxes was emperor of Persia, there was a man named Ezra. He traced his ancestors back to Aaron, the High Priest.

Ezra was a scholar with a thorough knowledge of the Law which the Lord, the God of Israel, had given to Moses.

Because Ezra had the blessing of the Lord his God, the emperor gave him everything he asked for.

In the **seventh** year of the reign of Artaxerxes, Ezra set out from Babylonia to Jerusalem with a group of Israelites.
They left Babylonia on the first day of the first month, and with God's help they arrived in Jerusalem on the
first day of the fifth month.
Ezra had devoted his life to studying the Law of the Lord, to practicing it, and to teaching all its laws and
regulations to the people of Israel.

Artaxerxes gave the following document to Ezra, the priest and scholar:

From Artaxerxes the emperor, to Ezra the priest, scholar in the Law of the God of Heaven.

"I command that throughout my empire all the Israelite people, priests and Levites, that so desire be permitted to go
with you to Jerusalem.
*I, together with my **seven** counselors, send you to investigate the conditions in Jerusalem and Judah in order to see how*

well the Law of your God, which has been entrusted to you, is being obeyed. You are to take with you the gold and silver

offerings which I and my councilors desire to give to the God of Israel, whose Temple is in Jerusalem. You are also to

take all the silver and gold which you collect throughout the province of Babylon and the offerings which the Israelite

people and their priests give for the Temple of their God in Jerusalem.

You are to spend this money carefully and buy bulls, rams, lambs, corn and wine, and offer them on the altar of the

Temple in Jerusalem.

You may use the silver and gold that is left over for whatever you and your fellow-countrymen desire, in accordance with

the will of your God.

You are to present to God in Jerusalem all the utensils that have been given to you for use in the Temple services. And

anything else which you need for the Temple, you may get from the royal treasury.

I command all the treasury officials in the province of West Euphrates to provide promptly for Ezra, the priest and

scholar in the Law of the God of Heaven, everything he asks you for, up to a limit of 3,400 kilograms of silver, 10,000

kilograms of wheat, 2,000 litres of wine, 2,000 litres of olive oil, and as much salt as necessary.

You must be careful to provide everything that the God of Heaven requires for his Temple, and make sure that he is

never angry with me or with those who reign after me. You are forbidden to collect any taxes from the priests, Levites,

musicians, guards, workmen or anyone else connected with this Temple.

You, Ezra, using the wisdom which your God has given you, are to appoint administrators and judges to govern all the

people in the West Euphrates who live by the Law of your God.

You must teach that Law to anyone who does not know it.

If anyone disobeys the Law of your God or the laws of the Empire, he is to be punished promptly: by death or by exile or

by confiscation of his property or by imprisonment."

[1] This story is taken from Ezra Chapter 7

Esther [1]

From his royal throne in Persia's capital city of Susa, King Xerxes ruled over one hundred and twenty _seven_

provinces, all the way from India to Sudan.

In the third year of his reign he gave a banquet for all his officials and administrators.

The armies of Persia and Media were present, as well as the governors and noblemen of the provinces. For six whole months he made a show of the riches of the imperial court with all its splendor and majesty. After that, the king gave a banquet for all the men in the capital city of Susa, rich and poor alike.

It lasted **_seven_** days and was held in the gardens of the royal palace.

The courtyard there was decorated with blue and white cotton curtains, tied by cords of fine purple linen to silver
rings on marble columns.
Couches made of gold and silver had been placed in the courtyard, which was paved with white marble, red
feldspar, shining mother-of-pearl, and blue turquoise.

Drinks were served in gold cups, no two were alike and the king was generous with the royal wine.

There were no limits on the drinks; the king had given orders to the palace servants that everyone could have
as much as he wanted.

Meanwhile inside the palace, Queen Vashti was giving a banquet for the women.

On the **_seventh_** day of his banquet the king was drinking and feeling merry, so he called in the **_seven_** eunuchs who
were his personal servants:

- Mehuman
- Biztha
- Harbona
- Bigtha
- Abagtha
- Zethar
- Carkas

He ordered them to bring in Queen Vashti, wearing her royal crown.

The queen was a beautiful woman and the king wanted to show off her beauty to the officials and all his guests.

But when the servants told Queen Vashti of the king's command, she refused to come. That made the king furious.

Now it was the king's custom to ask for expert opinion on questions of law and order, so he called for his
advisers, who would know what should be done.

Those he most often turned to for advice were:
- Carshena
- Shethar

- Admatha

- Tarshish

- Meres

- Marsena

- Memucan

Seven officials of Persia and Media who held the highest offices in the kingdom. He said to these men,

"I, King Xerxes, sent my servants to Queen Vashti with a command, and she refused to obey it! What does the Law say we should do with her?"

Then Memucan declared to the king and his officials,

"Queen Vashti has insulted not only the king but also his officials — in fact, every man in the empire! Every woman in the empire will begin to look down on her husband as soon as she hears what the queen has done.

They'll say,

'King Xerxes commanded Queen Vashti to come to him and refused.' When the wives of the royal officials of Persia and Media hear about the queen's behavior they will be telling their husbands about it before the day is out. Wives everywhere will have no respect for their husbands, and husbands will be angry with their wives. If it pleases Your Majesty, issue a royal proclamation that Vashti may never again appear before the king. Order it to be written in the Laws of Persia and Media, so it can never be changed. Then give her place as queen to a better woman. When your proclamation is made known all over this huge empire, every woman will treat her husband with proper respect, whether he is rich or poor."

The king and his officials liked this idea, and the king did what Memucan suggested. To each of the royal provinces he sent a message in the language and system of writing of that province, saying that every husband should be the master of his home and speak with final authority.

Later, even after the king's anger had cooled down, he kept thinking about what Vashti had done and about his proclamation against her.

So some of the king's advisers who were close to him suggested,

"Why don't you search to find some beautiful young virgins? You can appoint officials in every province of the empire and order them to bring young girls to your harem here in Susa, the capital city. Put them in the care of Hegai, the eunuch who is in charge of your women, and let them be given a beauty treatment. Then take a girl you like best and make her queen in Vashti's place."

The king thought it was good advice and followed it.

There in Susa lived a Jew named Mordecai son of Jair; he was from the tribe of Benjamin and was a descendant of Kish and Shimei.

He had a cousin Esther, whose Hebrew name was Hadassah; she was a beautiful girl, and had a good figure.

At the death of her parents, Mordecai had adopted her and brought her up as his own daughter.

When the king had issued his new proclamation and many girls were being brought to Susa, Esther was among them.

She too was put in the royal palace in the care of Hegai, who had charge of the harem. Hegai liked Esther and she won his favor.

He lost no time in beginning her beauty treatment of massage and a special diet.

He gave her the best place in the harem and assigned ___seven___ girls specially chosen from the royal palace to serve her.

The time came for Esther to see the king. Esther was admired by everyone who saw her. When it was her turn to see the king, she wore just what Hegai advised her to wear.

So in Xerxes' ___seventh___ year as king, Esther was brought to him in the royal palace.

The king liked her more than any of the other girls, and more than any of the others she won his favor and affection.

He placed the royal crown on her head and made her queen in place of Vashti.

[1] This story is taken from Esther Chapters 1-2

<u>Proverbs</u> [1]

There are <u>**seven**</u> things that the Lord hates and cannot tolerate:-
- A proud look.
- A lying tongue.
- Hands that kill innocent people.
- A mind that thinks up wicked plans.
- Feet that hurry off to do evil.
- A witness who tells one lie after another.
- A man that stirs up trouble among friends.

*"The <u>**seven**</u> deadly sins are also known as the capital vices or cardinal sins and function as a grouping and classification*
of major vices within the teachings of Christianity and Islam.

*According to the standard list, the <u>**seven**</u> deadly sins in Christianity are:*
- *Pride*
- *Greed*
- *Wrath*
- *Envy*
- *Lust*
- *Gluttony*
- *Sloth*

In Islam these are:
- *Shirk (idolatry or polytheism)*
- *Witchcraft*
- *Usury (the lending of money at exorbitant interest rates)*
- *Disrespect of parents*
- *Fornication*
- *Unjust accusation against women*
- *Unjust murder*

(Wikipedia)

Wisdom has built her house and made **_seven_** pillars for it. She has had an animal killed for a feast, mixed spices
in the wine and laid the table.

She has sent her servant girls to call out from the highest
place in the town: "Come in, ignorant people!"

And to the foolish man she says,

"Come, eat my food and drink the wine that I have mixed.
Leave the company of ignorant people, and live.

Follow the way of knowledge."
If you correct a conceited man, you will only be insulted. If you reprimand an evil man, you will only get hurt. Never correct a conceited man — he will hate you for it. But if you correct a wise man, he will respect you. Anything you say to a wise man will make him wiser. Whatever you tell a righteous man will add to his knowledge.

To be wise you must first obey the Lord.

If you know the Holy One, you have understanding. Wisdom will add years to your life.

You are the one who will profit if you have wisdom, and if you reject it, you are the one who will suffer.

Stupidity is like a loud, ignorant, shameless woman. She sits at the door of her house or on a seat in the highest part of town and calls out to people passing by, who are minding their own business:

"Come in, ignorant people!" To the foolish man she says,

"Stolen water is sweeter. Stolen bread tastes better."

Her victims do not know that the people die who go to her house, that those who have already entered are now deep in the world of the dead.

[1] This story is taken from Proverbs Chapter 6 & 9

A warning to the Women of Jerusalem [1]

The Lord said,
"Look how proud the women of Jerusalem are!

They walk along with their noses in the air. They are always flirting. They take dainty little steps, and the
bracelets on their ankles jingle.

But I will punish them — I will shave their heads and leave them bald."

A day is coming when the Lord will take away from the women of Jerusalem everything they are so proud of

— the ornaments they wear on their ankles, on their heads, on their necks, and on their wrists. He will take away
their veils and their hats; the magic charms they wear on their arms and their waists; the rings they wear on their
fingers and in their noses; all their fine robes, gowns, cloaks, and purses; their revealing garments, their linen
handkerchiefs and their scarves and long veils they wear on their heads.
Instead of using perfumes, they will stink; Instead of fine belts, they will wear coarse ropes; Instead of having
beautiful hair, they will be bald; Instead of fine clothes, they will be dressed in rags; their beauty will be turned
to shame.
The men of the city, yes, even the strongest men, will be killed in war. The city gates will mourn and cry and the
city itself will be like a woman sitting on the ground, stripped naked.

When the time comes, **_seven_** women will grab hold of one
man and say,

"We can feed and clothe ourselves, but please let us say you are our
husband, so that we won't have to endure the
shame of being unmarried."

[1] This story is taken from Isaiah Chapter 3 & 4

—— God will Bless his people [1]

You people who live in Jerusalem will not weep any more.

The Lord is compassionate and when you cry to him for help
— he will answer you.

The Lord will make you go through hard times, but he himself will be
there to teach you, and you will not have
to search for him any more.

If you wander off the road to the right or the left, you will
hear his voice behind you saying, "Here is the road. **Follow
it!!!!"**

You will take your idols plated with silver and your idols covered
with gold, and will throw them away like filth,
shouting,

"OUT OF MY SIGHT!"

Whenever you sow your seeds, the Lord will send rain to make
them grow and will give you a rich harvest, and
your cattle will have plenty of pasture. The oxen and donkeys that
plough your fields will eat the finest and best
fodder.
On the day when the forts of your enemies are captured and their
people are killed, streams of water will flow
from every mountain and every hill.

The moon will be as bright as the sun, and the sun will be
seven times brighter than usual, like the light of

<u>*seven*</u> days in one.

This will all happen when the Lord bandages and heals the wounds he has given his people.

[1] This story is taken from Isaiah Chapter 30

Then the Lord said to me,

"Even if Moses and Samuel were standing here pleading with me, I would not show these people any mercy.

Make them go away; make them get out of my sight. When they ask you where they should go; tell them what I
have said:

Some are doomed to die by disease — That is where they will go!

Others are doomed to die in war — That is where they will go!

Some are doomed to die of starvation — That is where they will go!

Others are doomed to be taken away as prisoners — That is where they will go!

I, the Lord, have decided that four terrible things will happen to them:

- they will be killed in **war**
- their bodies will be dragged off by dogs
- birds will eat them
- wild animals will devour what is left over

I will make all the people of the world horrified at them because of what Hezekiah's son Manasseh did in
Jerusalem when he was king of Judah."

The Lord says,

"Who will pity you, people of Jerusalem, And who will grieve over you?

Who will stop long enough To ask how you are?

You people have rejected me;

You have turned your back on me.

So I stretched out my hand and crushed you Because I was tired of controlling my anger. In every town in the land

I threw you to the wind like straw I destroyed you, my people,

I killed your children

Because you did not stop your evil ways.

There are more widows in your land

Than grains of sand by the sea.

I killed your young men in their prime

And made their mothers suffer.

I suddenly struck them With anguish and terror.

*The mother who lost her **seven** children has fainted, Gasping for breath.*

Her daylight has turned to darkness.

She is disgraced and sick at heart.

I will let your enemies kill

Those of you that are still alive.

I, the Lord, have spoken.“

¹ This story is taken from Jeremiah Chapter 15

___Babylonia [1]

On the tenth day of the fifth month of the nineteenth year of King Nebuchadnezzar of Babylonia, Nebuzaradan,

adviser to the king and commander of his army, entered Jerusalem.

He burnt down the Temple, the palace, and the houses of all the important people in Jerusalem; and his

soldiers tore down the city walls.

Then Nebuzaradan took away to Babylonia the people who were left in the city, the remaining skilled

workmen, and those who had deserted to the Babylonians.

But he left in Judah some of the poorest people, who owned no property and he put them to work in the vineyards

and fields.

In addition, Nebuzaradan, the commanding officer, took away as prisoners Seraiah the High Priest,

Zephaniah the priest next in rank, and the three other important temple officials.

From the city he took the officer who had been in command of the troops, ***seven*** of the king's personal advisers

who were still in the city, the commander's assistant, who was in charge of military records, and sixty other

important men.

Nebuzaradan took them to the king of Babylonia, who was in the city of Riblah in the territory of Hamath. There the king had them tortured and put them to death.

So the people of Judah were carried away into exile.

This is the record of the people that Nebuchadnezzar took away as prisoners:

In his **_seventh_** year as king he carried away 3,023; in his eighteenth year 832 and in his twenty third year, 745.

In all 4600 people were taken away.

[1] This story is taken from Jeremiah Chapter 51

Ezekiel [1]

God said to Ezekiel,

"Mortal man, pay close attention and remember everything I tell you. Then go to your countrymen who are

in exile and tell them what I, the Sovereign Lord, am saying to them, whether they pay attention to you or

not."

Then God's spirit lifted me up, and I heard behind me the loud roar of a voice that said, "PRAISE THE GLORY OF THE LORD IN HEAVEN ABOVE!"

I heard the wings of the animals beating together in the air, and the noise of the wheels, as loud as an earthquake.

The power of the Lord came on me with great force, and as his spirit carried me off, I felt bitter and angry.

So I came to Tel Abib beside the River Chebar, where the exiles were living, and for _seven_ days I stayed there overcome by what I had seen and heard.

After the _seven_ days had passed, the Lord spoke to me and said,

"Mortal man, I am making you a watchman for the nation of Israel. You must pass on to them the warnings I

give you. If I announce that an evil man is going to die but you do not warn him to change his ways so that he

can save his life, he will die, still a sinner, and I will hold you responsible for his death. If you do warn an evil

man and he doesn't stop sinning, he will die, still a sinner, but your life will be spared.

If a truly good man starts doing evil and I put him in a dangerous situation, he will die if you do not warn

him. He will die because of his sins — I will not remember the good he did — and I will hold you

responsible for his death. If you do warn a good man not to sin and he listens to you and doesn't sin, he

will stay alive, and your life will also be spared."

[1] This story is taken from Ezekiel Chapter 3

Daniel's Three Friends [1]

The king of Babylonia, Nebuchadnezzar, ordered his chief official to select from the Israelite exiles some young

men of the royal family and of the noble families.

They had to be handsome, intelligent, well-trained, quick to learn and free from physical defects.

After three years of special training, they appeared before the king. Among those chosen were Daniel, Hananiah, Mishael and Azariah.

They were renamed Belteshazzar, Shadrach, Meshach and Abednego by the chief official.

Daniel interpreted the king's dream after the king threatened to have all of his royal advisers to be executed.

The king rewarded Daniel by giving him many splendid gifts, putting him in charge of all the royal advisers and

in charge of the province of Babylon.

Daniel remained in the royal court and requested the king to put Shadrach, Meshach and Abednego in charge of

the affairs of the province of Babylon.

King Nebuchadnezzar had a gold statue made and instructed the people to bow down and worship the gold

statue, as soon as the music started.

As soon as they heard the sound of the instruments, the people of all the nations, races and languages bowed

down and worshipped the gold statue, which King Nebuchadnezzar had set up.

It was then that some Babylonians took the opportunity to denounce the Jews. They said to King Nebuchadnezzar,

"May your Majesty live forever! Your Majesty has issued an order that as soon as the music starts, everyone is
to bow down and worship the gold statue and anyone that does not bow down and worship it is to be thrown
into a blazing furnace. There are some Jews whom you put in charge of the province of Babylon — Shadrach,
Meshach and Abednego — who are disobeying Your Majesty's orders. They do not worship your god or bow
down to the statue you set up."

At that, the king flew into a rage and ordered the three men
to be brought before him. He said to them,

"Shadrach, Meshach and Abednego, is it true that you refuse to worship my god and to bow down to the gold
statue that I have set up? Now then as soon as you hear the sounds of the trumpets, oboes, lyres, zithers, harps,
and all the other instruments, bow down and worship the statue. If you do not, you will immediately be thrown
into a blazing furnace.

Do you think that there is any god that can save you?"

Shadrach, Meshach and Abednego answered,

"Your Majesty, we will not try to defend ourselves. If the God whom we serve is able to save us from the
blazing furnace and from your power, then he will. But even if he doesn't, Your Majesty may be sure that we
will not worship your god, and we will not bow down to the gold statue that you have set up."

Then Nebuchadnezzar lost his temper, and his face turned red with anger at Shadrach, Meshach and

Abednego.

So he ordered his men to heat the furnace seven times hotter than usual.

And he commanded the strongest men in his army to tie the three men up and throw them in the blazing

furnace.

So they tied them up, fully dressed — shirts, robes, caps and all — and threw them into the blazing furnace.

Now because the king had given strict orders for the furnace to be made **_seven_** times hotter, the flames

burnt up the guards who took the men to the furnace.

Then Shadrach, Meshach and Abednego, still tied up, fell into the heart of the blazing fire.

Suddenly Nebuchadnezzar leapt to his feet in amazement. He asked his officials,

"Didn't we tie up the three men and throw them into the blazing furnace?" They answered,

"Yes, we did, Your Majesty."

"Then why do I see four men walking about in the fire?" He asked. "They are not tied up and they show no

sign of being hurt — and the fourth one looks like a god."

So Nebuchadnezzar went up to the door of the blazing furnace and called out, "Shadrach! Meshach!

Abednego! Servants of the Supreme God! Come Out!"

And they came out at once.

All the princes, governors, lieutenant-governors, and the other officials of the king gathered to look at the

three men who had not been harmed by the fire.

Their hair was not burnt, their clothes were not burnt and there was no smell of smoke on them.

The king said,

"Praise the God of Shadrach, Meshach and Abednego! He sent his angel and rescued these men who serve

and trust him. They disobeyed my orders and risked their lives rather than bow down and worship any god

except their own.

And now I command that if anyone of any nation, race or language speaks disrespectful of the God of

Shadrach, Meshach and Abednego, he is to be torn limb from limb, and his house is to be made a pile of

ruins. There is no other god that can rescue like this!"

And the king promoted Shadrach, Meshach and Abednego to higher positions in the province of Babylon.

[1] This story is taken from Daniel Chapter 1-3

Nebuchadnezzar's Second Dream [1]

King Nebuchadnezzar sent the following message to the people of all nations, races and languages of the

world:

"Greetings!

Listen to my account of the wonders and miracles which the Supreme God has shown me.

How great are the wonders God shows us. How powerful are the miracles he performs? God will be king forever.

He will rule for all time!

I was living comfortably in my palace, enjoying great prosperity.

But I had a frightening dream and saw terrifying visions while I was asleep.

I ordered all the Royal advisors in Babylon to be brought to me so that they could tell me what the dream meant.

Then all the fortune-tellers, magicians, wizards, and astrologists were brought in, and I told them my dream, but they could not explain it to me.

Then Daniel came in.

The spirit of the Holy God is in him. I told him what was in my dream,

"Daniel, I know that the spirit of the Holy God is in you and that you understand all mysteries.

This is my dream.

Tell me what it means.

While I was asleep, I had a vision of a huge tree in the middle of the earth. It grew bigger and bigger until it reached the
sky and could be seen by everyone in the world. Its leaves were beautiful and it was loaded down with fruit — enough
for the whole world to eat. Wild animals rested in its shade, birds build nests in its branches, and every kind of living
being ate its fruit.

While I was thinking about the vision, I saw an angel coming down from heaven, alert and watchful. He proclaimed in a loud voice,

'CUT THE TREE DOWN AND CHOP OFF ITS BRANCHES. STRIP OFF ITS LEAVES AND SCATTER ITS FRUIT. DRIVE THE ANIMALS FROM UNDER IT AND THE BIRDS OUT OF ITS BRANCHES. BUT LEAVE THE STUMP IN THE GROUND WITH A BAND OF IRON AND BRONZE AROUND IT. LEAVE IT THERE IN THE FIELD WITH GRASS. NOW LET THE DEW FALL ON THIS MAN, AND LET HIM LIVE WITH THE ANIMALS AND THE PLANTS. FOR SEVEN YEARS HE WILL NOT HAVE A HUMAN MIND, BUT THE MIND OF AN ANIMAL. THIS IS THE DECISION OF THE ALERT AND WATCHFUL ANGELS. SO THEN, LET ALL THE PEOPLE EVERYWHERE KNOW THAT THE SUPREME GOD

HAS POWER OVER HUMAN KINGDOMS AND THAT HE CAN GIVE THEM TO ANYONE HE CHOOSES — EVEN TO THE LEAST IMPORTANT OF MEN.'

This is the dream I had.

Now, Daniel, tell me what it means.

None of my royal advisors could tell me, but you can, because the spirit of the Holy God is in you."

Daniel replied,

"Your Majesty, I wish that the dream and its explanation applied to your enemies and not to you. Your Majesty, you are the tree, tall and strong!

You have grown so great that you reach the sky. Your power extends over the whole world.

This is what the Supreme God has declared will happen to you. You will be driven away from human society.

You will live with wild animals.

*For **seven** years you will eat grass like an ox, and sleep in the open air, where dew will fall on you.*

Then you will admit that the Supreme God controls all human kingdoms, and that he can give them to anyone he chooses.

The angels ordered the stump to be left in the ground.

This means that you will become king again when you acknowledge that God rules the world. So then, Your Majesty, follow my advice.

Stop sinning. Do what is right.

Be merciful to the poor.

Then you will continue to be prosperous."

All of this did happen to King Nebuchadnezzar.

Only 12 months later, while he was walking around on the roof of his royal palace in Babylon he said, "Look how great Babylon is! I built it as my capital city to display my power and my might, my glory and

my majesty!"

Before the words were out of his mouth, a voice spoke from heaven, "King Nebuchadnezzar, listen to what I say!

Your royal power is now taken away from you. You will be driven away from human society. You will live with wild animals.

You will eat grass like an ox for <u>seven</u> years. Then you will acknowledge that the

Supreme God has power over human kingdoms. He can give them to anyone he chooses."

The words became true immediately.

Nebuchadnezzar was driven out of human society and ate grass like an ox.

The dew fell on his body and his hair grew as long as eagles' feathers and his nails as long as birds' claws.

*"When the **seven** years had passed," said the king, "I looked up at the sky and my sanity returned. I praised the Supreme God and gave honor and glory to the one who lives forever.*

He will rule forever.

And his kingdom will last for all time.

He looks on the people of the earth as nothing.

Angels in heaven and people on earth are under his control. No one can oppose his will.

Or Question what he does.

And now, I, Nebuchadnezzar, praise, honor, and glorify the King of Heaven. Everything he does is right and just.

He can humble anyone who acts proudly."

[1] *This story is taken from Daniel Chapter 4*

<u>Zechariah</u> [1]

Zechariah was a prophet who lived in the year 520 B.C

He received messages from God in visions at night....

In another vision the Lord showed me the High Priest Joshua standing before the angel of the Lord.

And there besides Joshua stood Satan (A supernatural being whose name indicates he was regarded as man's

opponent), ready to bring an accusation against him.

"Then I heard a loud voice in heaven saying, 'Now God's salvation has come!

Now God has shown his power as King! Now his Messiah has shown his authority! For the one who stood before our God And accused our brothers day and night Has been thrown out of heaven." (Revelations 12:10)

The angel of the Lord said to Satan, "May the Lord condemn you, Satan!
May the Lord who loves Jerusalem, condemn you.
This man is like a stick snatched from the fire."

Joshua was standing there wearing filthy clothes. The angel said to his heavenly attendants,

"Take away the filthy clothes this man is wearing." Then the angel said to Joshua,

"I have taken away your sin and will give you new clothes to wear." He commanded the attendants to put a clean turban on Joshua's head.

They did so, and then they put the new clothes on him while the angel of the Lord stood there. Then the angel told Joshua that the Lord Almighty had said,

"If you obey my laws and perform the duties I have assigned to you, then you will continue to be in charge of my

Temple and its courts, and I will hear your prayers, just as I hear the prayers of the angels who are in my

presence. Listen then, Joshua, you who are the High Priest, and listen, you fellow-priests of his, you that are a

sign of a good future:

I will reveal my servant, who is called The Branch! I am placing in front of Joshua a single stone with _**seven**_

facets. I will engrave an inscription on it, and in a single day, I will take away the sin of this land.

When that day comes, each of you will invite his neighbor to come and enjoy peace and security, surrounded by

your vineyards and fig-trees."

[1] This story is taken from Zechariah Chapter 3

Anna [1]

Joseph went from the town of Nazareth in Galilee to the town of Bethlehem in Judaea, the birthplace of King
David.

Joseph went there because he was a descendant of David.

He went to register with Mary, who was promised in marriage to him.

She was pregnant, and while they were in Bethlehem, the time came for her to have her baby. She gave birth to her first son, wrapped him in strips of cloth and laid him in a manger.

The time came for Joseph and Mary to perform the ceremony of purification as the Law of Moses commanded.

So they took the child to Jerusalem to present him to the Lord, as it is written in the law of the Lord, "Every first-born male is to be dedicated to the Lord"

They also went to offer a sacrifice of a pair of doves or two young pigeons, as required by the law of the Lord.

At that time there was a man named Simeon living in Jerusalem. He was a good, devout man and was waiting for Israel to be saved.

The Holy Spirit was with him and had assured him that he would not die before he had seen the Lord's
promised Messiah.

Led by the spirit, Simeon went into the Temple.

When the parents brought the child Jesus into the Temple to do for him what the Law required, Simeon took
the child in his arms and gave thanks to God:

"Now, Lord, you have kept your promise, And you may let your servant go in peace. With my own eyes I have seen your salvation, Which you have prepared in the presence

Of all peoples.

A light to reveal your will to the Gentiles And bring glory to your people Israel."

The child's father and mother were amazed by the things Simeon said about him. Simeon blessed them and said to Mary, his mother,

"This child is chosen by God for the destruction and the salvation of many in Israel. He will be a sign from God
which many people will speak against and so reveal their secret thoughts. And sorrow, like a sharp sword, will
break your own heart."

There was a very old prophetess, a widow named Anna, daughter of Phanuel of the tribe of Asher. She had been married for only _**seven**_ years and was now 84 years old.

She never left the Temple; day and night she worshipped God, fasting and praying.

That very same hour she arrived and gave thanks to God and spoke about the child to all who were waiting for God to set Jerusalem free.

When Joseph and Mary had finished doing all that was required by the law of the Lord, they returned to their hometown of Nazareth in Galilee.

The child grew and became strong; he was full of wisdom and God's blessings were upon him.

[1] This story is taken from Luke Chapter 2

Beelzebub [1]

Jesus was driving out a demon that could not talk and when the demon went out, the man began to talk. The crowds were amazed, but some of the people said,

"It is Beelzebub, the chief of the demons, who gives him the power to drive them out."

Others wanted to trap Jesus, so they asked him to perform a miracle to show that God approved of him. But Jesus **knew** what they were thinking, so he said to them,

"Any country that divides itself into groups which fight each other, will not last very long. A family divided
against itself falls apart. So if Satan's kingdom has groups fighting each other, how can it last? You say that I
drive out demons because Beelzebub gives me the power to do so. If this is how I drive them out, how do your
followers drive them out? Your own followers prove that you are wrong! No, it is by means of God's power that I
drive out demons, and this proves that the Kingdom of God has already come to you. When a strong man, with
all his weapons ready, guards his own house, all his belongings are safe. But when a stronger man attacks him
and defeats him, he carries away all the weapons the owner was depending on and divides up what he stole.
Anyone who is not for me is really against me; anyone who does not help me gather is really scattering.
When an evil spirit goes out of a person, it travels over dry country looking for a place to rest. If it can't find one,
it says to itself,

'I will go back to my house.'

So it goes back and finds the house clean and tidy.

Then it goes out and brings **_seven_** other spirits even worse than itself, and they come and live there. So when it is all over, that person is in a worse state than he was at the beginning."

[1] This story is taken from Luke Chapter 11

The Question about Rising from Death [1]

Some Sadducees, who say that people will not rise from the death, (For the Sadducees say that people will not

rise from death and there are no angels or spirits - Acts 23:8) came to Jesus and said,

"Teacher, Moses wrote the Law for us:

'If a man dies and leaves his wife but no children, that man's brother must marry the widow so that they can have

children who will be considered the dead man's children.'
Once there were *seven* brothers; the eldest got married and died without having children. Then the second one

married the woman, and then the third. The same thing happened to all *seven*

— they died without having children. Last of all the woman died. Now, on that day that the dead rise to life, whose

wife will she be? All *seven* of them had married her."

Jesus answered them,

"The men and women of this age marry, but the men and women who are worthy to rise from death and live in

the age to come will not then marry. They will be like angels and cannot die. They are the sons of God, because

they have risen from death. And Moses clearly proves that the dead are raised to life. In the passage about the

burning bush he speaks of the Lord as,

'The God of Abraham, the God of Isaac and the God of Jacob'

He is the God of the living not of the dead, for to him all are alive."

Some of the teachers of the Law spoke up, "A good answer, Teacher!"

For they did not dare to ask him any more questions. [1] This story is taken from Luke Chapter 20

___*Seven* Disciples [1]

In his disciples' presence Jesus performed many other miracles which are not written down in this book.

But these have been written in order that you may believe that Jesus is the Messiah, the Son of God, and that
through your faith in him you may have life.

After this, Jesus appeared once more to his disciples at Lake Tiberias. This is how it happened.

Simon Peter,

Thomas (called the Twin)

Nathanael (the one from Cana in Galilee) The two sons of Zebedee

And two other disciples of Jesus were all together.

___*Seven* in total.

Simon Peter said to the others, "I am going fishing."
"We will come with you," they told him.

So they went out in a boat, but all that night they did not catch a thing.

As the sun was rising, Jesus stood at the water's edge, but the disciples did not know that it was Jesus. Then Jesus asked them,

"Young men, haven't you caught anything?" "Not a thing," they answered.

Jesus said to them,

"Throw your net out on the right side of the boat, and you
will catch some."

So they threw the net out and could not pull it back in,
because they had caught so many fish.

The disciple whom Jesus loved said to Peter, "It is the Lord!"

When Peter heard that it was the Lord, he wrapped his outer
garment around him (for he had taken his clothes
off) and jumped into the water.

The other disciples came to shore in the boat, pulling the
net full of fish. They were not very far from land, about a
hundred metres away.

When they stepped ashore, they saw a charcoal fire there
with a dish on it and some bread. Then Jesus said to them,

"Bring some of the fish you have just caught."

Simon Peter went aboard and dragged the net ashore full of big
fish, a hundred and fifty three in all; even though
there were so many, still the net did not tear.
Jesus said to them, "Come and eat."
None of the disciples dared ask him, "Who are you?"
Because they knew it was the Lord.
So Jesus went over, took the bread and gave it to them; he did the
same with the fish.
This, then, was the third time Jesus appeared to the disciples after
he was raised from the dead.
[1] This story is taken from John Chapter 21

____The *Seven* Helpers [1]

The Council of all the Jewish elders called the apostles in, had them whipped, and ordered them never again to

speak in the name of Jesus; and then they set them free.

As the apostles left the Council they were happy, because God had considered them worthy to suffer disgrace for

the sake of Jesus.

And every day in the Temple and in people's homes they continued to teach and preach the Good News about

Jesus the Messiah.....

As the number of disciples kept growing, there was a quarrel between the Greek-speaking Jews and the native

Jews.

> The Greek-speaking Jews claimed that their widows were being neglected in the daily distribution of funds. So the twelve apostles called the whole group of believers together and said,

> "It is not right for us to neglect the preaching of God's word in order to handle the finances.

So then, brothers, choose **_seven_** men among you who are known to be full of the Holy Spirit and wisdom, and we

will put them in charge of this matter. We, ourselves, then, will give our full time to prayer and the work of

preaching."

> The whole group was pleased with the apostles' proposal, so they chose: Stephen - a man full of faith and the Holy Spirit

Philip Prochorus Nicanor Timon Parmenas

Nicolaus - a Gentile from Antioch who had earlier been converted to Judaism

The group presented themselves to the apostles, who prayed and placed their hands on them. And so the Word of God continued to spread.

The numbers of disciples in Jerusalem grew larger and larger, and a great number of priests accepted the

faith.

[1] This story is taken from Acts Chapter 6

The Sons of Sceva [1]

God was performing unusual miracles through Paul.

Even handkerchiefs and aprons he had used were taken to those who were ill, and their diseases were driven
away, and the evil spirits would go out of them.
Some Jews who traveled round and drove out evil spirits also tried to use the name of the Lord Jesus to do this.

They said to the evil spirits,
"I command you in the name of Jesus, whom Paul preaches."

Seven brothers, who were the sons of a Jewish High Priest named Sceva, were doing this. But the evil spirit said to them,

"I know Jesus, and I know about Paul, but you — who are you?"

The man who had the evil spirit in him attacked them with such violence that he overpowered them all. They ran away from his house, wounded and with their clothes torn off.

All the Jews and Gentiles who lived in Ephesus heard about this; they were all filled with fear, and the name of
the Lord Jesus was given greater honor.

Many of the believers came, publicly admitting and revealing what they had done.

Many of those who had practiced magic brought their books together and burnt them in public.

They added up the price of books, and the total came to 50,000 silver coins (A silver coin was the daily wage of a rural worker).

In this powerful way the Word of the Lord kept spreading and growing stronger! [1]This story is taken from Acts Chapter 19

______God's Mercy on Israel [1]

Paul wrote his letter to the Romans to explain his understanding of the Christian faith and its practical
implications for the lives of Christians.

Paul said that **all** mankind, both Jews and Gentiles, needs to be put right with God, for all alike are under the
power of sin. People are to be put right with God through faith in Jesus Christ.....

I ask, then: Did God reject his own people?

I myself am an Israelite, a descendant of Abraham, a member of the tribe of Benjamin. God has not rejected his people, whom he chose from the beginning.

You know what the scripture says in the passage where Elijah pleads with God against Israel:

"Lord, they have killed your prophets and torn down your altars; I am the only one left, and they are trying to kill
me."

What answer did God give him?

"I have kept for myself _**seven**_ thousand men who have not worshipped the false god Baal."

It is the same way now: there is a small number left of those whom God had chosen because of his grace, not on
what they have done.

For if God's choice was based on what people do, then his grace would not be real grace. What then?

The people of Israel did not find what they were looking for. It was only the small group that God chose who
found it; the rest grew deaf to God's call.

As the scripture says,

"God made their minds and hearts dull; to this very day they cannot see or hear." And David says,

"May they be caught and trapped at their feasts; May they fall, may they be punished!

May their eyes be blinded so that they Cannot see;

And make them bend under their Troubles at all times."

I ask, then:

When the Jews stumbled, did they fall to their ruin? By no means! Because they sinned, salvation has come to
the Gentiles, to make the Jews jealous of them.
The sin of the Jews brought rich blessings to the world, and their spiritual poverty brought rich blessings to the
Gentiles.

Then, how much greater the blessings will be when the complete number of Jews is included!

[1] This story is taken from Romans Chapter 11

Revelations

<u>Greetings to the _seven_ churches</u> (Chapter 1)
From John to the **_seven_** churches in the province of Asia:

Grace and peace be yours from God, who is, who was and who is to come, and from the _seven_ spirits in front of
his throne, and from Jesus Christ, the faithful witness, the first to be raised from death and who is also the
ruler of the kings of the world.
He loves us, and by his death he has freed us from our sins, and made us a kingdom of priests to serve his God
and Father. To Jesus Christ be the glory and power for ever and ever!
Amen.

Look, he is coming on the clouds!

Everyone will see him, including those who pierced him. All peoples on earth will mourn over him.

So shall it be!

"I am the first, and the last," says the Lord God Almighty, who is, who was and who is to come.

<u>A vision of Christ</u> (Chapter 1)

I am John, your brother, and as a follower of Jesus I am your partner in patiently enduring the suffering that
comes to those who belong to his Kingdom.

I was put on the island of Patmos because I had proclaimed God's word and the truth that Jesus had revealed. On the Lord's day the Spirit took control of me, and I heard a loud voice, that sounded like a trumpet,

speaking behind me.

It said,

"Write down what you see, and send the book to the churches in these **_seven_** cities: Ephesus, Smyrna, Pergamum, Thyatira, Sardis, Philadelphia and Laodicea."

I turned round to see who was talking to me, and I saw **_seven_** gold lamp-stands, and among them there was
what looked like a human being, wearing a robe that reached to his feet, and a gold belt round his chest. His hair
was white as wool or as snow, and his eyes blazed like fire; his feet shone like brass that had been refined and
polished, and his voice sounded like a roaring waterfall.

He held **_seven_** stars in his right hand, and a sharp two-edged sword came out of his mouth. His face was as bright as the midday sun.

When I saw him, I fell down at his feet like a dead man. He placed his right hand on me and said,

"Don't be afraid! I am the first and the last! I am the living one! I was dead but now I am alive for ever and
ever. I have authority over death and the world of the dead (It was thought that the dead continued to exist in
a dark world under the ground).

Write, then, the things you see, both the things that are now and the things that will happen afterwards. This

is the secret meaning of the **_seven_** stars that you see in my right hand, and of the seven gold lamp-stands:

The **_seven_** stars are the angels of the **_seven_** churches. The seven lamp-stands are the seven churches.

Worship in heaven (Chapter 4)

At this point I had another vision and saw an open door in heaven.

And the voice that sounded like a trumpet, which I had heard speaking to me before, said, "Come up here, and

I will show you what must happen after this."

At once the Spirit took control of me.

There in heaven was a throne with someone sitting on it.

His face gleamed like such precious stones as jasper and carnelian, and all round the throne there was a

rainbow the color of an emerald.

In a circle round the throne were 24 other thrones, on which were seated 24 elders dressed in white and

wearing crowns of gold.

From the throne came flashes of lightning, rumblings and peals of thunder.

In front of the throne **_seven_** lighted torches were burning, which are the seven spirits of God. Also in front of

the throne there was what looked like a sea of glass, clear as crystal.

Surrounding the throne on each of its sides, were four living creatures covered with eyes in front and behind.

The first one looked like a lion;

The second looked like a bull;

The third had a face like a man's face; The fourth looked like an eagle in flight.

Each one of the four living creatures had six wings, and they were covered with eyes, inside and out. Day and night they never stopped singing:

"Holy, holy, holy, is the Lord God Almighty, Who was, who is and who is to come."

The four living creatures sing songs of glory and honor and thanks to the one who sits on the throne, who

lives for ever and ever.

When they do so, the 24 elders fall down before the one who sits on the throne, and worship him who lives for

ever and ever.

They throw their crowns down in front of the throne and say, "Our Lord and God!

You are worthy to receive glory, honor & power. For you created all things,

And by your will they were given existence & life."

The Scroll and the Lamb (Chapter 5)

I saw the scroll in the right hand of the one who sits on the throne; it was covered with writing on both sides

and was sealed with _**seven**_ seals.

And I saw a mighty angel who announced in a loud voice,

"WHO IS WORTHY TO BREAK THE SEALS AND OPEN THE SCROLL?"

But there was no one in heaven or on earth or in the world below (the world of the dead) who could open the

scroll and look inside it.

I cried bitterly because no one could be found who was worthy to open the scroll or look inside it. Then one of

the elders said to me,

"Don't cry. Look! The Lion from Judah's tribe, the great descendant of David, has won the victory, and he can

break the _**seven**_ seals and open the scroll."

Then I saw a Lamb standing in the centre of the throne, surrounded by the four living creatures and the elders.

The Lamb appeared to have been killed.

It had **_seven_** horns and **_seven_** eyes, which are the **_seven_** spirits of God that have been seen throughout the

whole earth.

The Lamb went and took the scroll from the right hand of the one who sits on the throne. As he did so, the

four living creatures and the 24 elders fell down before the Lamb.

Each had a harp and gold bowls filled with incense, which are the prayers of God's people.

They sang a new song,

"You are worthy to take the scroll And to break open its seals.

For you were killed, and by your death You bought for God

People from every tribe, language, Nation and race.

You have made them a kingdom of Priests to serve our God,

And they shall rule on earth."

Again I looked, and I heard angels, thousands and millions of them!

They stood round the throne, the four living creatures, and the elders, and sang in a loud voice:

"THE LAMB WHO WAS KILLED IS WORTHY

TO RECEIVE POWER, WEALTH, WISDOM AND STRENGTH,

HONOR, GLORY AND PRAISE!"

And I heard every creature in heaven, on earth and in the world below — all living beings in the universe —

and they were singing:

"To him who sits on the throne and To the Lamb,

Be praise and honor, glory and might, For ever and ever!"

The four living creatures answered, "Amen!"

And the elders fell down and worshipped.

The _Seventh_ seal (Chapter 8)

When the Lamb broke open the **_seventh_** seal, there was silence in heaven for about half an hour.

Then I saw the _seven_ angels who stand before God, and they were given _seven_ trumpets. Another angel, who had a gold incense-burner, came and stood at the altar.

He was given a lot of incense to add to the prayers of all God's people and to offer it on the gold altar that
stands before the throne.
The smoke of the burning incense went up with the prayers of God's people from the hands of the angel standing
before God.

Then the angel took the incense-burner, filled it with fire from the altar, and threw it on the earth. There were rumblings and peals of thunder, flashes of lightning and an earthquake.

___**The Trumpets** (Chapter 8)
Then the _seven_ angels with the _seven_ trumpets prepared to blow them.

The first angel blew his trumpet.

Hail and fire, mixed with blood, came pouring down on the earth. A third of the earth was burnt up, a third of the
trees, and every blade of green grass.

Then the second angel blew his trumpet.

Something that looked like a huge mountain on fire was thrown into the sea. A third of the sea was turned
into blood, a third of the living creatures in the sea died, and a third of the ships were destroyed.

Then the third angel blew his trumpet.

A large star, burning like a torch, dropped from the sky and fell on a third of the rivers and on the springs of
water. (The name of the star is "Bitterness"). A third of the water turned bitter, and many people died from
drinking the water, because it had turned bitter.

Then the fourth angel blew his trumpet.

A third of the sun was struck, and a third of the moon, and a third of the stars, so that their light lost a third of
its brightness; there was no light during a third of the day and a third of the night.

Then the fifth angel blew his trumpet.

I saw a star which had fallen down to the earth, and it was given the key to the abyss (the place in the depths of
the earth where the demons were imprisoned until their final punishment).
The star opened the abyss, and smoke poured out of it, like the smoke from a large furnace; the sunlight and
the air were darkened by the smoke from the abyss.
Locusts came down out of the smoke upon the earth, and they were given the same power that the scorpions
have. They were told not to harm the grass or the trees or any other plant; they could harm only the people who
did not have the mark of God's seal on their foreheads. The locusts were not allowed to kill these people, but
only to torture them for five months. The pain caused by the torture is like the pain caused by a scorpion's

sting. During those five months they will seek death, but will not find it; they will want to die, but death will

flee from them.

The locusts looked like horses ready for battle; on their heads they had what seemed to be crowns of gold, and

their faces were like men's faces. Their hair was like women's hair, their teeth were like lions' teeth. Their

chests were covered by what looked like iron breastplates, and the sound made by their wings was like the

noise of many horse-drawn chariots rushing into battle. They have tails and stings like those of a scorpion, and

it is with their tails that they have the power to hurt people for five months.

They have a king ruling over them, who is the angel in charge of the abyss.

His name in Hebrew is Abaddon; in Greek the name is Apollyon (meaning "The Destroyer). The first horror is over.

The sixth angel blew his trumpet.

I heard a voice coming from the four corners of the gold altar standing before God. The voice said to the sixth angel,

"Release the four angels who are bound at the great river Euphrates!"

The four angels were released; for this very hour of this very day of this very month and year they had been kept ready to kill a third of all mankind.

I was told the number of mounted troops - it was two hundred million. And in my vision I saw the horses and their riders:

They had breastplates red as fire, blue as sapphire and yellow as sulphur.

Their horses' heads were like lions' heads, and from their mouths came out fire, smoke and sulphur. A third of mankind was killed by those three plagues: fire, smoke and sulphur.

For the power of the horses is in their mouths and also in their tails. Their tails are like snakes with heads, and they use them to hurt people.

The rest of mankind, all those who had not been killed by these plagues, did not turn away from what they themselves had made.

They did not stop worshipping demons, nor the idols of gold, silver, bronze, stone, and wood, which cannot see, hear or walk.

Nor did they repent of their murders, their magic, their sexual immorality, or their stealing.

The Angel and the Little Scroll (Chapter 10)

Then I saw another mighty angel coming down out of heaven.

He was wrapped in a cloud and had a rainbow round his head; his face was like the sun, and his legs were like pillars of fire.

He had a small Scroll open in his hand.

He put his right foot on the sea and his left foot on the land, and called out in a loud voice that sounded like the roar of lions.

After he called out, the seven thunders answered with a roar. As soon as they spoke, I was about to write.

But I heard a voice speak from heaven,

"Keep secret what the seven thunders have said; do not write it down."

Then the angel that I saw standing on the sea and on the land raised his right hand to heaven, and took a vow in the name of God, who lives forever and ever, who created heaven, earth and the sea, and everything in them. The angel said,

"There will be no more delay! But when the seventh angel blows his trumpet, God will accomplish his secret plan, as he announced to his servants, his prophets."

Then the voice I had heard speaking from heaven spoke to me again saying,

"Go and take the open scroll which is in the hand of the angel standing on the sea and the land." I went to the angel and asked him to give me the little scroll.

He said to me,

"Take it and eat it; it will turn sour in your stomach but in your mouth it will be as sweet as honey." I took the little scroll from his hand and ate it, and it tasted sweet as honey in my mouth.

But after I swallowed it, it turned sour in my stomach. Then I was told,

"Once again you must proclaim God's message about many nations, races, languages and kings."

The *Seventh* Trumpet (Chapter11)

Then the seventh angel blew his trumpet, and there were loud voices in heaven, saying,

"THE POWER TO RULE OVER THE WORLD BELONGS NOW TO OUR LORD AND HIS MESSIAH, AND HE WILL RULE FOREVER AND EVER."

God's temple in heaven was opened, and the Covenant Box was seen there.

Then there were flashes of lightning, rumblings and peals of thunder, an earthquake, and heavy hail.

The Woman and the Dragon (Chapter 12)

Then a great and mysterious sight appeared in the sky.

There was a woman, whose dress was the sun and who had the moon under her feet and a crown of twelve stars on her head.

She was soon to give birth, and the pains and suffering of childbirth made her cry out.

Another mysterious sight appeared in the sky. There was a huge red dragon with seven heads and ten horns and a crown on each of his heads.

With his tail he dragged a third of the stars out of the sky and threw them down to the earth. He stood in front of the woman, in order to eat her child as soon as it was born.

Then she gave birth to a son, who will rule over all nations with an iron rod. But the child was snatched away and taken to God and his throne.

The woman fled to the desert, to a place God had prepared for her, where she will be taken care of for 1,260 days.

Then war broke out in heaven. Michael and his angels fought against the dragon, who fought back with his angels; but the dragon was defeated, and he and his angels were not allowed to stay in heaven any longer.

The huge dragon was thrown out — that ancient Serpent called the Devil, or Satan, that deceived the whole world.

He was thrown down to earth, and all his angels with him.

Then I heard a loud voice in heaven saying,

"Now God's salvation has come! Now God has shown his power as King! Now his Messiah has shown his authority! For the one who stood before God and accused our brothers day and night, has been thrown out of heaven.

Our brothers won the victory over him by the blood of the Lamb and by the truth which they proclaimed; and they were willing to give up their lives and die. And so be glad, you heavens, and all you that live there! But how terrible for the earth and the sea! For the Devil has come down to you, and he is filled with rage, because he knows that he has only a little time left."

When the dragon realized that he had been thrown down to earth, he began to pursue the woman who had given birth to the boy. She was given the two wings of a large eagle in order to fly to her place in the desert,

where she will be taken care of for three and a half years, safe from the dragon's attack.

And then from his mouth the dragon poured out a flood of water after the woman, so that it would carry her away. But the earth helped the woman, it opened its mouth and swallowed the water that had come from the dragon's mouth. The dragon was furious with the woman and went off to fight against the rest of her descendants, all those who obey God's commandments and are faithful to the truth revealed by Jesus.

And the dragon stood on the sea-shore.

<u>The two beasts</u> (Chapter 13)

Then I saw a beast coming up out of the sea.

It had ten horns and seven heads; on each of its horns was a crown; and on each of its seven heads was a name that was insulting to God.

The beast looked like a leopard, with feet like a bear's feet and a mouth like a lion's mouth. The dragon gave the beast his own power, his throne, and his vast authority.

One of the heads of the beast seemed to have been fatally wounded, but the wound had healed. The whole earth was amazed and followed the beast. Everyone worshipped the dragon because he had given his authority to the beast. They worshipped the beast also, saying,

"Who is like the beast? Who can fight against it?"

The beast was allowed to make proud claims which were insulting to God, and it was permitted to have authority for 42 months.

It began to curse God, his name, the place where he lives, and all those who live in heaven.

It was allowed to fight against God's people and to defeat them, and it was given authority over every tribe, nation, language and race. All people living on earth will worship it, except those whose names were written before the creation of the world in the book of the living which belongs to the Lamb who was killed.

"Listen, then if you have ears! Whoever is meant to be captured, will surely be captured; whoever is meant to be killed by the sword will surely be killed by the sword. This calls for endurance and faith on the part of God's people."

<u>The Angels with the Last Plagues</u> (Chapter 15)

Then I saw in the sky another mysterious sight, great and amazing.

There were seven angels with seven plagues, which are the last ones, because they are the final expression of God's anger.

Then I saw what looked like a sea of glass mixed with fire. I also saw those who had won the victory over the beast and its image and over the one whose name is represented by a number.

They were standing by the sea of glass, holding harps that God had given them and singing the song of Moses, the servant of God, and the song of the Lamb:

"Lord God Almighty

How great and wonderful are your deeds!

King of the nations

How right and true are your ways!

Who will not fear you, Lord?

Who will refuse to declare your greatness?

You alone are Holy.

All the nations will come and worship you

Because your just actions are seen by all."

After this I saw the Temple in heaven open, with the Tent of God's presence in it.

The seven angels who had the seven plagues came out of the Temple, dressed in clean shining linen and with gold belts tied around their chests.

Then one of the four living creatures gave the seven angels seven gold bowls full of the anger of God, who lives forever and ever.

The Temple was filled with smoke from the glory and power of God, and no one could go into the Temple until the _**seven**_ plagues brought by the _**seven**_ angels had come to an end.

The Bowls of God's Anger (Chapter 16)

Then I heard a loud voice speaking from the Temple, to the seven angels:

"Go and pour out the _**seven**_ bowls of God's anger on the earth!"

The first angel went and poured his bowl on the earth.

Terrible and painful sores appeared on those who had the mark of the beast and on those who had worshipped his

image.

Then the second angel poured out his bowl on the sea.

The water became like the blood of a dead person, and every living creature in the sea died.

Then the third angel poured out his bowl on the rivers and the springs of water, and they turned into blood.

Then the fourth angel poured out his bowl on the sun, and it was allowed to burn people with its fiery heat. They were burnt by the fierce heat, and they cursed the name of God, who has authority over these plagues. But they would not turn from their sins and praise his greatness.

Then the fifth angel poured out his bowl on the throne of the beast.

Darkness fell over the beast's kingdom, and people bit their tongues because of their pain, and they cursed the

God of Heaven for their pains and sores.

But they did not turn from their evil ways.

Then the sixth angel poured out his bowl on the great river Euphrates. The river dried up, to provide a way for

the kings who came from the east. Then I saw three unclean spirits that looked like frogs. They were coming out

of the mouth of the dragon, the mouth of the beast, and the mouth of the false prophet. They are the spirits of

demons that perform miracles. These three spirits go out to all the kings of the world, to bring them together for the battle on the Great Day of the Lord Almighty!

"Listen! I am coming like a thief! Happy is he that stays awake and guards his clothes, so he will not walk around naked and be ashamed in public!"

Then the spirits brought the kings together in the place that in Hebrew is called Armageddon.

Then the **_seventh_** angel poured out his bowl in the air. A loud voice came from throne in the Temple, saying,

"It is done."

There were flashes of lightning, rumblings and peals of thunder, and a terrible earthquake.

There has never been such an earthquake since the creation of man; this was the worst earthquake of all! The great city was split into three parts, and the cities of all countries were destroyed.

God remembered great Babylon and made her drink the wine from his cup — the wine of his furious anger. All the islands disappeared and all the mountains vanished.

Huge hailstones, each weighing as much as 50 kilos, fell from the sky on people, who cursed God on account of
the plague of hail, because it was such a terrible plague.

<u>The Famous Prostitute</u> (Chapter 17)
Then one of the <u>*seven*</u> angels who had the <u>*seven*</u> bowls came
to me and said,

"Come, and I will show you how the famous prostitute is to be punished, that great city that is built near many
rivers. The kings of the earth practiced sexual immorality with her, and the people of the world became drunk
from drinking the wine of her immorality."

The Spirit took control of me, and the angel carried me to a desert.

There I saw a woman sitting on a red beast that had names insulting to God written all over it; the beast had _seven_ heads and ten horns.

The woman was dressed in purple and scarlet, and covered with gold ornaments, precious stones and pearls.

In her hand she held a gold cup full of obscene and filthy things, the result of her immorality.

On her forehead was written a name that has a secret meaning:

"Great Babylon, the mother of all the prostitutes and perverts in the world."

And I saw that the woman was drunk with the blood of God's people and the blood of those who were killed because they had been loyal to Jesus.

When I saw her, I was completely amazed. "Why are you amazed?" The angel asked me.

"I will tell you the secret meaning of the woman and of the beast that carries her, the beast with _seven_ heads and ten horns. The beast was once alive, but lives no longer; it is about to come up from the abyss and will go off to be destroyed. The people living on earth whose names have not been written before the creation of the world in the book of the living, will be amazed when they look at the beast. It was once alive; now it no longer lives but it will reappear. This calls for wisdom and understanding. The _seven_ heads are _seven_ hills, on which the woman sits. There are also _seven_ kings: five of them have fallen, one still rules and the other one has not yet come; when he comes, he must rule only a little while. And the beast that was once alive, but lives no longer, is itself an

eighth king who is one of the _seven_ and is going off to be destroyed. The ten horns you saw are ten kings who

have not yet begun to rule, but who will be given authority to rule as kings for one hour with the beast. These ten

all have the same purpose, and they give their power and authority to the beast. They will fight against the

Lamb, together with his called, chosen, and faithful followers, and will defeat them, because he is the Lord of

lords and King of kings.

The angel also said to me,

"The waters you saw, on which the prostitute is sitting, are nations, peoples, races and languages. The ten

horns you saw, and the beast, will hate the prostitute; they will take away everything she has and leave her

naked; they will eat her flesh and destroy her with fire.

For God has placed in their hearts the will to carry out his purpose by acting together and giving the beast their

power to rule until God's words come true.

The woman you saw is the great city that rules over the kings of the earth."

So be it.

Come, Lord Jesus!

May the grace of the Lord Jesus be with

everyone.

(Revelations 22:20-21)

www.ingramcontent.com/pod-product-compliance
Lightning Source LLC
Chambersburg PA
CBHW061439150726
47987CB00001B/273